CW00417354

Dochum Liam is Domhnaill

gean na fianaigheachta do dháileadar orm

The Fenian Cycle in Irish

and Scots-Gaelic Literature

Joseph J. Flahive

Cork Studies in Celtic Literatures 1

2017

Cork Studies in Celtic Literatures 1

The Fenian Cycle in Irish and Scots-Gaelic Literature

Joseph J. Flahive

2017

Series Editor: Kevin Murray

Editorial Board: John Carey, Emma Nic Cárthaigh, Caitríona Ó Dochartaigh

www.ucc.ie/en/cscl/

Published by Cork Studies in Celtic Literatures
ISBN: 978-0-9955469-0-5

*Published with the assistance of University College Cork's
CACSSS Research Publication Fund,*

Contents

Abbreviations

Manuscript Repositories

BLL	British Library, London
BLO	Bodleian Library, Oxford
NLI	The National Library of Ireland, Dublin
NLS	The National Library of Scotland, Edinburgh
RIA	Royal Irish Academy, Dublin
TCD	Trinity College, Dublin
UCD	University College, Dublin

Texts and Manuscripts

AcS *Acallam na Senórach* (earliest version, represented by the editions of Stokes and O'Grady; and the translations of O'Grady, Dooley and Roe, and Harmon).

AgS *Agallamh na Seanórach* (version in RIA MS 24 P 5 [93], also called *The Reeves Agallamh* and *An tAgallamh Déanach*; and citations from the edition of it by Ní Shéaghdha).

BDL Book of the Dean of Lismore / Leabhar an Deadhain / Leabhar Deathan Lios Mòir (NLS Adv. MS 72.1.37 [Gaelic MS XXXVII]; *olim* Highland Society MS John M'Kenzie 1).

BLis. Book of Lismore (Private possession of the Duke of Devonshire, Chatsworth House, Bakewell, Derbyshire).

DF Duanaire Finn (UCD Archives, Franciscan MS A20a; *olim* Killiney, Franciscan House of Studies MS A20) (Roman letters refer to the manuscript; when used in reference to the Irish Texts Society edition of MacNeill and Murphy, it is italicised).

LL Book of Leinster / Leabhar Laighean (TCD MS H.2.18 [1339]) (Roman letters refer to the manuscript; when used in reference to the diplomatic edition of Best et al., it is italicised).

LU Lebor na hUidre (RIA MS 23 E 25 [1229]) (Roman letters refer to the manuscript; when used in reference to the diplomatic edition of Best and Bergin, it is italicised).

LUM Leabhar Ua Maine (RIA Stowe MS D ii 1 [1225]).

YBL Yellow Book of Lecan / Leabhar Buidhe Leacáin (TCD MS H.2.16 [1318]).

Introduction

This work is intended as a handbook to the traditional Fenian literature of Ireland and Scotland from the earliest times to the modern period. As a synthesis for the use of student and layman alike, it follows in the footsteps of Gerard Murphy, whose booklet *The Ossianic Lore and Romantic Tales of Medieval Ireland* still retains its value after sixty years. This modest guide has many worthy predecessors, of which a few ought to be credited at the outset. Alfred Nutt's groundbreaking *Ossian and the Ossianic Literature* (which does not concern Macpherson's Ossian despite its title) for the first time constructed a coherent chronological account of the development of the corpus of medieval Fenian literature, which pioneering scholars such as Whitley Stokes and Kuno Meyer had begun to edit and translate. Kuno Meyer's *Fianaigecht* combined editions and translations of a number of key texts with the first attempt to list and categorise linguistically the portion of the corpus composed before the fourteenth century. Gerard Murphy, prior to writing his aforementioned guide, set the study of Fenian literature on a scientific grounding as part of his introduction to *Duanaire Finn* (iii, pp. xi–lxxxvii, §§2–10).

Where the present work chiefly differs from earlier introductions is in the footnotes: I have attempted to name the major Fenian texts and collections, and to cite all major texts and text collections and modern scholarship on them as a bibliographical guide. Although it is impossible to cite every text edition, especially eighteenth- and nineteenth-century publications of lays or ballads, or to delineate definitively where the present subject crosses over into folklore, Anglo-Irish or Scottish literature, or comparative literary studies, it has been necessary to extend slightly beyond the strict boundaries of the enquiry.

In the decades following the publication of *Duanaire Finn* and the editions of a large number of prose *fianaigheacht* tales, most especially by Nessa Ní Shéaghdha, a generation passed in which the Fenian Cycle fell from academic fashion, despite the efforts of scholars such as Ann Dooley, Donald E. Meek, Joseph F. Nagy, Máirtín Ó Briain, and Seán Ó Coileáin. The last few years have seen surging interest in this literature, accompanied by the appearance of many publications including the proceedings of the first *Fianaigecht* Conference in Cambridge, edited by Sharon Arbuthnot and Geraldine Parsons as *The Gaelic Finn Tradition* (the proceedings of the second conference in Glasgow are in preparation), and the colloquium on the *Agallamh* tradition in

the originally assigned limitations, and scholarship of the last few years has been taken into account, but the basic concept has not changed.

The roots of this study, however, lie deeper. I examined the evolution of the Fenian verse tradition through to the opening of the Early Modern period in Chapters 2–3 of my doctoral thesis, 'The Relic Lays: A Study in the Development of Late Middle-Gaelic *Fianaigheacht*' (University of Edinburgh, 2004), and the foundations of my interest in and exploration of the vast Fenian corpus lie there. I must give my especial thanks to William Gillies and Donald E. Meek, under whose expert supervision I began these studies.

Additional thanks are due to Seán Ó Coileáin for reading and commenting on an earlier version of this study, and to two external readers for their careful evaluation of the work. Its transformation into the present volume is due to the request and insistence of Kevin Murray, in addition to his assistance with the draft and many helpful suggestions (including drawing my attention to many useful references), not to mention his keen proof-reading. Were it not for his perseverance, this work would not have appeared at all. I wish to thank the members of the Departments of Modern Irish and Early and Medieval Irish, University College Cork, with whom I have discussed this material over a number of years. They have pointed out to me a number of references to enrich this study and made many helpful suggestions. I have received great assistance from the staff of Special Collections in the Boole Library, where much of this volume was written. Finally, I could not have undertaken this task without the continual support of my wife, Bernadette McCarthy. All remaining faults are mine.

Standardisation

Since this work covers fifteen hundred years of literature, extending from Old Irish to Modern Irish, Scots Gaelic, and Manx, the spelling of Classical Modern Irish will be used throughout for names and terms appearing in the body-text for reasons of consistency; where Old and Middle Irish forms differ significantly, they will be given in parentheses.[1] Forms of the word *fian* 'warrior

---

[1] Old Irish covers the period 600–900 AD; Middle Irish 900–1200 AD; Classical Modern Irish 1200–1650 AD (this is the poetic register; the spoken and lower written register of the same period is called Early Modern Irish); Modern Irish 1650–present.

band' (plural *fiana*) and related terms are spelt here with a single *n*, the more historically correct spelling of the root; present-day usage, as well as some earlier scribes, use spellings with *–nn*; arguments regarding the correct spelling of some *fian-* compounds are on-going, but a consensus regarding the word *féinidh* / *féinnidh* has emerged in favour of the latter form. The Early Modern form of its plural (*féinnidhthe*), which continues in Modern Irish, has been preferred to the original *i*-stem (*féinnidi*) with which it co-existed in the Middle Ages.

The names of tales and poems bring other issues of presentation to the fore. The original Irish and Scots-Gaelic forms of these names, linked with the time and place of their creation, cannot be standardised, but must be presented in the form in which they are preserved, especially when they constitute the titles of published editions. Translations of these have been provided. Some texts have been named, in Irish or English, by their editors and translators. Such editorial titles in Irish have been retained. When the name of a poem or tale has not been translated by its editor, a literal translation has been supplied in brackets, but non-literal renderings of text names in English, where commonly used, have been allowed to stand. The same procedure has been followed throughout in regard to the first lines of poems lacking titles. In the cases of a few texts published with an English-language title only, these are retained, though an *incipit* with translation is provided as appropriate.

All citations of Irish and Scots-Gaelic texts have been printed as they appear in the editions. Translations accompanying the texts cited (or occasionally later translations based on the same edition, as noted) have been used when possible, though with slight adjustments for reasons of consistency, and with correction of tense where nineteenth-century translators misunderstood the *s*-preterite as a narrative present. Translations have been supplied by the present author where none is available.

Both shelfmarks and catalogue numbers (bracketed) are provided in the first citations of all NLS, RIA, and TCD manuscripts because they are encountered in published scholarship (regardless of the libraries' present practices), but the shelfmarks stand alone in short citations thereafter. For other libraries, the shelfmark generally suffices; older numberings and customary manuscript names are provided as necessary.

In order to avoid confusion, the term Ossianic is avoided except in relation to James Macpherson's creations and their close affiliates (Chapter Seven), although it appears as a synonym for the Fenian / Fionn Cycle in quotations drawn from older scholar-ship, where it is allowed to stand. Finally, terms such as Fenian Cycle and *fianaigheacht* have been conflated in indexing to avoid the separation of thematically similar material.

1. The Roots of the Cycle

An Fhianaigheacht, the Fenian Cycle, is also known as the Fionn Cycle and (especially in Scotland) as the Ossianic Cycle. Of all the cycles of Gaelic literature — for it is a literature of Scots Gaelic as well as of Irish – *fianaigheacht* has been productive the longest, from the earliest vernacular writings to the present, and its corpus is by far the largest. The literature primarily concerns adventures of the *fian*, or warband, led by Fionn mac Cumhaill. In one Middle Irish reference in the *dinnsheanchas* ('place lore') of Carmun, heading a list of literary subjects, this topic is already described as *Fian-śruth Find, fáth cen dochta*, 'Tales of Find and the Fianna, a matter inexhaustible'.[1]

Before embarking on a description of content, it is proper to ask what constitutes a cycle and thus to define more precisely the matter under investigation. The concept, at least in a vague sense, has been a part of medieval literary criticism for well over a century, initially and most frequently invoked in regard to the multi-authored, multi-national, and multi-lingual Arthurian literature. Erich Poppe has explored what comprises a cycle more specifically in the Insular context, finding three criteria for definition: that a group of texts are connected by the description of the same 'world'; that any text in the group 'must cohere with at least one other text' in regard to characters, and to setting in time and place; and that there are shared references between texts.[2] The medieval tale-lists, however, arrange the early Irish stories quite differently, according to their themes, mixing the tales of distinct heroes such as Fionn, Cú Chulainn, Lugh, and the Kings; this has given rise to queries as to how the authors of the tales understood them.[3] For the present purposes, two points are noted: first, that the early term *fian-śruth* seems to denote this literature as defined by character-related content, and *fianaigheacht* comes to assume this meaning; secondly, Poppe's criteria are fully met by the materials that these terms describe in Irish and Scots Gaelic through the centuries (and by some English-language compositions of more recent times), but not by Macpherson's Ossian and its close relations which comprise a 'world' of their own.[4]

Academic opinion, as well as the living tradition, once held

---

[1] Gwynn, *The Metrical Dindshenchas*, iii, 20.
[2] Poppe, *Of Cycles and Other Critical Matters*, 3–14, esp. the defining qualities at 10–11.
[3] See Mac Cana, *The Learned Tales of Medieval Ireland*.
[4] See Chapter Seven below.

that Fionn and his *fian* were historical warriors around whom legendary accretions collected (see Chapter Six). In the course of scholarly investigation, a consensus began to emerge in the early twentieth century that Fionn has his origins in a god, who has been euhemerised, that is, adapted as a human hero. *Vindos* 'the White / Fair' is the ancient Celtic word from which the Irish name Fionn (earlier Find) derives. In continental inscriptions, the practice of pairing native names of gods with Roman deities with similar attributes or functions preserves the name VINDONNOS as an equivalent to Apollo; it has been suggested that this is a diminutive form of *Vindos*.[5] Gerard Murphy lists a number of place-names, including Vendres, France; Windisch, Switzerland; and Vienna, Austria, all of which, he argues, contain the name of this god.[6] Recently, however, several scholars have raised doubts.[7] They would view Fionn as a purely legendary figure, lacking religious roots as well as historical ones. Nevertheless, it is unquestionable that the figure of Fionn has deep roots in the Insular tradition, whatever conclusions may be reached about the figure of *Vindos*. The Welsh hero Gwynn ap Nudd not only has a cognate name, but also shares a mythological name in his supposed pedigree in common with the Irish Fionn — the ancestral deity *Nōdons* (whence Irish Nuadu, later Nuadha; Welsh Nudd) — and is presented in medieval Welsh literature as an heroic hunter figure like the Irish Fionn.[8]

In the earliest literature, Fionn, whether euhemerised from a hero-god or originating as a legendary mortal, is presented as a

---

[5] See Hirschfeld and Zangmeister, *Corpus Inscriptionum Latinarum XIII*, 105, §§5644–6.

[6] Murphy, *The Ossianic Lore*, 8; further discussion of the name types by Murphy may be found in *DF* iii, pp. lxxxii–iv.

[7] Tomás Ó Cathasaigh re-appraised the deity of Fionn in 'Cath Maige Tuired as Exemplary Myth'; therein, he observed that in Irish literature 'Lug is a divine hero, whereas Finn is not: Lug is a hero among the gods ... whereas Finn dies, and when he is dead he is dead' (p. 13). Building on these observations, John Carey has raised the question of whether the scant inscriptional evidence has been interpreted correctly ('Nōdons, Lugus, Windos', 109), in effect questioning whether there was any such god among the continental Celts. The toponymic interpretation of the element *uindo–* has been adjectival ('white, bright, open') rather than personal in the recent work of Falileyev, *The Dictionary of Continental Celtic Place Names*, 34–5 (cf. discussion of other names containing this element, especially those in *Vind–*, pp. 238–9).

[8] For discussion of the Welsh Gwynn and his parallels with Fionn, see Carey, 'Nōdons, Lugus, Windos', 110–17.

2

hero and poet with Otherworldly powers of prophecy. *Macgním-artha Finn* ('The Boyhood Deeds of Fionn'), described below, confirms Fionn's conformity to the heroic template in regard to his birth and early life.[9] Attempts to reconstruct a mythological Fionn have been further complicated by the assimilation of parts of the myths of Lugh, the hero-god of the Mythological Cycle, into the life of Fionn. Despite many a scholar's valiant attempts, it appears impossible to establish definitively whether parallels between these figures are due to a common template for a hero-god, direct borrowing from one to the other, or a more complex cross-fertilisation, though it is likely that all these processes played some part.[10] Fionn's great rival, Aodh mac Morna, usually called Goll, is a one-eyed man with a name meaning 'fire'; his rivalry with Fionn is analogous to — or borrowed from — the myth of Lugh and Balor, the latter of whom is a one-eyed arsonist.[11] Other major characters and plots of the cycle also contain varying degrees of what is not unlikely to be a mythological residue.[12] Regardless of the extent of the mythological contribution, there is a widespread element of magic in the literature, particularly in regard to certain characteristics of Fionn as a seer.[13]

The legendary life of Fionn, however, is presented with a fair degree of consistency throughout the literature and is summar-

---

[9] The Fionn of the *Macgnímartha* has been the subject of a full monograph: Nagy, *The Wisdom of the Outlaw*; see also Scowcroft's review 'On Liminality in the Fenian Cycle'. Another full-length study of the character of Fionn is Ó hÓgáin, *Fionn mac Cumhaill: Images of the Gaelic Hero*; the core element of Fionn's heroic character is addressed more succinctly in idem, 'Fionn Féin — Pearsa agus Idéal'.

[10] It should be no surprise that T.F. O'Rahilly, the first scholar to explore the parallels in such heroic Irish figures as Cormac mac Airt, Fionn, Cú Chulainn, and Lugh, finally concluded that there was in fact only one figure, a single Celtic Ur-hero (*Early Irish History and Mythology*, 271–81, 318–40); this view has been championed more recently by Carney, 'Language and Literature to 1169', 488: 'Once the identity of Lug and Finn is accepted, the former can be used to build up the primitive Celtic picture of the latter'. Most scholars, whilst noting the strong correspondence, would shrink from O'Rahilly's conclusion; for example, Mac Cana, 'Fianaigecht in the Pre-Norman Period', 79, 83–4. The parallels between Lugh and Fionn are evaluated at length in Ó Cathasaigh, '*Cath Maige Tuired*', and Carey, 'Nōdons, Lugus, Windos'. Nagy has explored the heroic template, especially in regard to parallels between Fionn and Cú Chulainn in 'Heroic Destinies in the *Macgnímrada* of Fionn and Cú Chulainn'.

[11] For discussion, see *DF* iii, pp. lxviii–lxxiii.

[12] Ibid., intro. §9, especially pp. lxx–lxxx.

[13] Ó hÓgáin, 'Magic Attributes of the Hero'.

ised with relative ease. Rising from an obscure childhood, Fionn defeats Ailléan, the monstrous burner of Tara, and thereby comes to be the chief leader of the *fiana* of Ireland, the post that he learns had been held by his father Cumhall. He reclaims his mother's hereditary home, the Hill of Allen (Irish *Almha*) in Co. Kildare, and makes it his stronghold.[14] Fionn holds his post for many years. Among the women with whom he is associated are Ailbhe and Gráinne, both daughters of high-king Cormac mac Airt, deepening his complicated links to the kingship of Tara. His son Oisín and grandson Oscar grow to manhood during the years of his leadership. There are innumerable stories that focus on the adventures of the *fian* and its warriors, some of whom achieve the status of heroic protagonist of individual tales and poems. Yet a conflict lurks under the surface throughout: Goll mac Morna had slain Cumhall in the battle of Cnucha and assumed headship of the *fian*, yet had made peace with Fionn and retained his place in the *fian* as an officer and as leader of the Clann Mhorna faction of Fionn's warriors. Eventually, under the influence of external pressures, this truce fails; the resulting strife destroys the *fian* in a series of battles — culminating in the battle of Gabhair with Fionn's *fian* on one side and Clann Mhorna and high-king Cairbre Lifeachair on the other — leaving only a few survivors. There are different traditions regarding Fionn's own death, either by the machinations of Goll's descendants, or by attempting in old age to re-enact an heroic leap that he had accomplished in his youth.[15] Among the last survivors are Oisín and his cousin Caoilte; beginning in the Middle Irish period and with increasing frequency, the literature is presented in the form of their reminiscences.[16]

It must be stressed, however, that although the literature implies knowledge of Fionn's biography, only a small portion of the corpus narrates the events described above. Rather, it usually describes adventures unconnected with the basic progression of the cycle such as hunts, battles with invaders, or encounters with the *aos sídhe* ('Otherworld dwellers'). When central events, such as the final battles of Gabhair and Ollarbha are narrated, they are

---

[14] For an account of the Hill of Allen in the literature, see Parsons, 'Revisiting Almu in Middle Irish Texts'.

[15] These varying accounts and their overlap are explored by Parsons, 'Breaking the Cycle? Accounts of the Death of Finn'.

[16] Despite the central role of Oisín, who often eclipses Fionn, his character has been the subject of surprisingly little study of the sort that is often applied to his father. The early portion of his life has been examined by Ó Briain, 'Oisín's Biography: Conception and Birth'.

told as discrete tales: the sense of a continuous plot central to the whole cycle, which Gerard Murphy termed 'the residuum proper to Fionn',[17] primarily resides in the audience's own structuring of the events in reference to the life of Fionn, to which any number of additional adventures may be affixed. The background knowledge expected of the readers of this literature hints at the size and strength of a parallel oral tradition throughout the productivity of the cycle, vestiges of which remain today.[18]

A mortal Fionn required not merely a biography but also a place in the unified scheme of Irish history and pseudo-history. The placement of the Fenian Cycle in the reigns of Cormac mac Airt and his son Cairbre Lifeachair in the third century AD is not attested until the Middle Irish period, and there are clear signs that the official chronology was not always observed. Obituaries of Fionn appear in two chronicles, but these entries reflect later synthesis rather than older tradition.[19] In the Cycles of the Kings, there is a body of Old Irish tales about Cormac mac Airt; Fionn almost never appears in these.[20] Furthermore, there are a few scattered mentions of Fionn in medieval Irish legal manuscripts, and numerous references to Cormac, yet Fionn and Cormac never appear together in this context. On the other hand, Cormac appears in a number of Fenian texts.[21] He is briefly mentioned in the Old Irish story *Bruiden Átha hÍ* ('The Contention of Áth Í'), while

---

[17] *DF* iii, p. xlv and discussed throughout §7 (pp. xlv–liv).

[18] See Poppe, *Of Cycles and Other Critical Matters*, 13–14; Clover, 'The Long Prose Form', 23–7. The Book of Howth (London, Lambeth Palace Library, Carew MS 623) provides another kind of evidence from the sixteenth century. Its Fenian texts, written in English, contain versions of tales that are not simply translations of the Irish literary tales but independent narration of events in the tradition, and more likely reflect the manner in which the tales were told at that time. The relationship of these texts with Irish literary versions is examined by Fischer, 'Fionn mac Cumhaill among the Old English: Some Comments on the Book of Howth'.

[19] Mac Airt and Mac Niocaill, *The Annals of Ulster*, 22–3, §116: *Find hua Boiscne decollatus est o Aichlech mc. Duibhdrenn ๅ o macaibh Uirgrend de Luaighnibh Temhrach oc Ath Brea for Boinn*, 'Find hua Boíscne was beheaded by Aichlech son of Dubdrenn and the sons of Uirgrend of the Luaigne of Temair at Áth Brea on the Boyne'. A parallel entry is included in *The Annals of Tigernach* (ed. and trans. by Stokes, *Revue Celtique* 17, 21).

[20] A notable exception is *Scéla Mosauluim*: see O Daly, *Cath Maige Mucrama*, 74–87, at 84–5.

[21] The grafting of these legends, along with fabrication of appropriate genealogy, is treated in McQuillan, 'Finn, Fothad, and *Fian*: Some Early Associations'.

5

'Finn and Gráinne' provides a glimpse of Cormac as the father of the ill-fated heroine in a text from the tenth or eleventh century.[22] In the Middle Irish tale *Tochmarc Ailbe* ('The Wooing of Ailbhe'), Fionn courts Ailbhe, another daughter of the great high-king, after the failed match with Gráinne.[23] At the close of the Middle Irish period, Cormac makes lengthier appearances in the earliest version of *Acallam na Senórach* (hereafter *AcS*; 'The Colloquy of the Ancients'), and lays VII and XLVII in *Duanaire Finn* (*DF*).[24] There are signs, purely internal to the Fenian Cycle, that hint at the artificiality of the chronology. Simplest among these are the prodigious lifespans of Oisín, Caoilte, and their few surviving Fenian followers. If Fionn is meant to have flourished in the third century, it is a stretch of chronology for his son and his nephew to discourse with Saint Patrick, who was held to have arrived in Ireland in 432 AD.[25] Nevertheless, the later tradition, in what may be its last major literary development of the legend, felt a need to justify Oisín's lifespan by an elongated visit to the Otherworld; two literary versions survive in verse as '*Laoidh Cholainn gan Chionn*' ('The Lay of the Headless Body') and '*Laoidh Oisín ar*

---

[22] *Bruiden Átha hÍ* is published by Meyer, 'Two Tales about Find', 242–5, from RIA Stowe MS D iv 2 (1223); from YBL and MS D iv 2 by Hull, 'Two Tales about Find', 323–9. 'Finn and Gráinne' is ed. and trans. by Meyer, 'Finn and Grainne'; ed. with German translation, Corthals, 'Die Trennung von Finn und Gráinne'. Regarding the date of the text, see Meyer, *Fianaighecht*, p. xxiii; Murphy, *DF* iii, p. lix; Corthals, 'Die Trennung', 73–5.

[23] Ed. and trans. into German by Thurneysen, 'Tochmarc Ailbe "Das Werben um Ailbe"'. Meyer (*Fianaigecht*, p. xxiv) assigned it to the tenth century, a judgement refined but not rejected by Thurneysen, who sensed other layers in its textual history ('Tochmarc Ailbe', 253). The riddling questions between the pair and their later independent circulation is discussed in Ó Cuív, 'Miscellanea 2: Agallamh Fhinn agus Ailbhe', and Innes, 'Fionn and Ailbhe's Riddles between Ireland and Scotland'.

[24] Ed. O'Grady from BLis. in *Silva Gadelica*, i, 94–233, trans. ii, 101–265; and ed. Stokes, 'Acallamh na Senórach', a critical edition with translations only of those passages not paralleled in O'Grady. Harmon, *The Dialogue of the Ancients*, provides a full translation of Stokes. Dillon presents a number of excerpts from the Irish text based on the Book of Lismore with normalised orthography and a full glossary in *Stories from the Acallam*. A recent translation, but based on a critical edition not yet published, is Dooley and Roe, *Tales of the Elders of Ireland*.

[25] Then again, Fionn, his son Oisín, and his grandson Oscar were all held by many of the same texts to have been warriors in their prime at the same time; and Goll served as an officer from before Fionn's birth through to the battle of Gabhair when Fionn was past his prime.

6

Thír na nÓg' ('The Lay of Oisín in the Land of Youth').[26] First appearing in the Fenian Cycle in *AcS* and becoming a feature of Early Modern lays and tales, we get the additional anachronism of introducing Lochlannaigh (Norsemen) as invading challengers for the *fiana*: Viking raiders first appeared historically in Ireland towards the end of the eighth century, five centuries after the supposed time of Fionn and his men.[27] This is not the sole anachronism in *AcS;* the high-king in the text is Diarmaid mac Cearbhaill, though the annals and other historical sources would have Laoghaire mac Néill reigning at that time, and none of the under-kings mentioned in *AcS* matches the names that one might expect from chronicles or genealogies.[28]

Though Fionn and his men are not historical, the *fian* was certainly a very real institution of early medieval Ireland, and *féinnidhthe* had defined roles in medieval Irish law. The Old Irish text *Tecosca Cormaic* ('The Instructions of Cormac') claims that 'everyone is a *féinnidh* [member of a *fian*] till he takes up husbandry' (*fénnid cách co trebad*); Meyer also includes clanless men and landless men as *féinnidhthe*.[29] It appears that, as in many early Indo-European societies, it was useful to put the hot blood of

---

[26] '*Laoidh Cholainn gan Chionn*' remains unpublished, but Máirtín Ó Briain discussed it and provided a list of the manuscripts in his article of that name (pp. 233–50). Further witnesses have been identified by Síle Ní Mhurchú, who is preparing an edition of the text. These move the *terminus ante quem* for the text's composition slightly earlier than Ó Briain suggested (thanks are due to Síle Ní Mhurchú for providing a copy of her unpublished paper, 'Editing *Agallamh Oisín agus Pádraig* and *Laoi Cholainn gan Cheann*', which she delivered at the International Congress of Celtic Studies in Glasgow, 2015). '*Laoidh Oisín ar Thír na nÓg*' is edited by An Seabhac, *Laoithe na Féinne*, 213–26. Earlier editions with English translations include Ó Flannghaile, *Laoi Oisín ar Thír na n-Óg* and O'Looney, '*Tír na nÓg*: The Land of Youth'. Discussion of these poems is provided by Ó Briain, 'Some Material on Oisín in the Land of Youth'.

[27] See Christiansen, *The Vikings and Viking Wars*, esp. 83–6 regarding *AcS*. For a more general account of the Vikings in Fenian literature, see Mac Cana, 'The Influence of the Vikings on Celtic Literature', esp. 97–112; and Christiansen, *The Vikings and Viking Wars*, 4–38. The Norse theme in the literature was the starting point for an ambitious, though never widely accepted theory, that Fionn's character is grounded in the historical Hiberno-Norse figure of Ketill Hvíti or Cattil Find; see Zimmer, 'Keltische Beiträge III'.

[28] See Dooley and Roe, *Tales*, pp. xx–xxi.

[29] Meyer, *The Instructions of King Cormac Mac Airt*, 46, §31.10 (with modified translation); idem, *Fianaigecht*, p. ix.

youth to work learning the arts of hunting and warfare, thereby relieving pressure on society until these men were required to take their fathers' places.[30] Richard Sharpe uncovered another aspect of the *fian*, that the term originally had connotations neutral or favourable to the institution in the oldest sources, but that churchmen who deplored their violence deliberately conflated *féinnidh* ('*fian*-member') and *díbhearg* ('brigand, reaver').[31] The Norse wars, which brought about the need to organise armies, probably caused the decline of the institution of the *fian* in the ninth century as the young warriors were diverted into larger, more formalised military units.[32] The heroism of Fionn and his warriors was not much celebrated in the literature (written largely by ecclesiastics), until well after the actual institution had ceased and the opposition of the Church waned over centuries. It is this early literature that is to be explored next.

---

[30] See McCone, 'Cúlra Ind-Eorpach na Féinne'; idem, 'Hund, Wolf und Krieger bei den Indogermanen'; idem, 'The Celtic and Indo-European origins of the *fian*'. A detailed comparison of the Irish and Ancient Greek customs is to be found in Enright, 'Fires of Knowledge'.

[31] Sharpe, 'Hiberno-Latin *Laicus*, Irish *Láech* and the Devil's Men'. See also McCone, 'Werewolves, Cyclopes, *Díberga* and *Fíanna*'.

[32] Binchy, 'The Passing of the Old Order', 122–3, 131. Another piece of evidence is to be found in *Immacallam in Dá Thuarad* (ed. and trans. by Stokes, as 'The Colloquy of the Two Sages'), a ninth-century text in which the cessation of the practice of *fíanaigheacht* is named (pp. 5–6, §235) as one of the signs of the end of the world in a list of omens of doomsday already manifest. Simms, however, has posited an earlier demise for institutionalised *fíanaigheacht*, arguing that the practice, being essentially pagan in character, faded away with the rise of Christianity, though some of the vocabulary was re-applied for brigands and mercenary warbands ('Gaelic Warfare in the Middle Ages', 100–6).

8

2. Fionn in Early Irish Literature

The Fenian Cycle, despite popular claims to the contrary, is reasonably well represented in materials originally composed in the Old and Middle Irish periods. There are many anecdotes, lists, and explanations belonging to the cycle, as well as tales and poems: Kuno Meyer made a list of early Irish Fenian items, of which he found fifty-four; the *Zeitschrift für celtische Philologie*'s reviewer of his work (probably himself!) identified a number more (without counting *dinnsheanchas* poems with a Fenian attribution in manuscript titles but no Fenian content).[1] Kevin Murray provides an up-to-date discussion of the basis for the early dates assigned to these texts by Meyer.[2] One may reasonably assume that there may be a few more early Fenian texts still lurking within the manuscript corpus, for they can hide in unlikely places, such as the *rosc* (passage of elevated language, frequently obscure) with prose introduction in which Fionn prophesies the arrival of Saint Fionnchú in the commentary on the *Martyrology of Óengus* in An Leabhar Breac.[3] An important fact lies at the root of the popular misconception of a paucity of early Fenian literature: less than half of Meyer's list consists of narrative or lyric literary texts. The perplexing references and brief passages that comprise so much of the list often present tantalising glimpses into the early treatment of Fionn and his warriors, but they presume an understanding of the background of the cycle. Although such items, for the most part, contain information of use for understanding the origins of the cycle, their contents are not literature. Puzzling glossary and commentary items often require further study to tease out the underlying narratives; this has been demonstrated by Sharon Arbuthnot in her recent study of the fragments relating to Fearcheas and the obscure *rincne*.[4] The literary portion of these items is a heterogenous mixture of prose and verse that hints at much of the later development of the corpus. This material is preserved

---

[1] Meyer, *Fianaigecht*, pp. xviii–xxxii; Anonymous, 'Review of Meyer, *Fianaigecht*', 599; an abridged translation (the review was in German) of these additions to Meyer's list has been inserted as an addendum to the 1993 reprint of *Fianaigecht*.

[2] 'Interpreting the Evidence: Problems with Dating the Early *Fianaigecht* Corpus'. See also Flahive 'The Relic Lays', 22–6.

[3] Item 33 of Meyer's list, from An Leabhar Breac (RIA MS 23 P 16 [1230]). The text is printed, with partial translation by Stokes, 'On the Calendar of Oengus', p. clxxii.

[4] 'Finn, Ferchess, and the *Rincne*'.

scattered through a number of manuscripts, but some of the largest collections are in LL and YBL; virtually all have been published, even if many of the earlier printed editions not infrequently failed to consider all manuscript witnesses now known. Several short tales in very old language are preserved independently in later manuscripts. 'Finn and the Man in the Tree' has been assigned to the eighth century by Kuno Meyer. It is found as an illustrative anecdote in a commentary on the *Senchas Már*.[5] Fionn chases Cúldubh, an Otherworld dweller who has snatched his dinner, and spears him at the door of the *síodh*. Fionn catches his hand in the door as a woman slams it shut on him. Fionn responds with an obscure rhetorical poem, which demonstrates that the Otherworldly knowledge belonging to the *síodh* has been imparted to him through his thumb. There is a second, originally distinct, part to the tale which then proceeds in another direction, taking on a version of the Biblical plot of Joseph and Potiphar's wife. Fionn has abducted a woman who falls in love with Fionn's servant Dearc Corra.[6] Fearing the wrath of Fionn, he refuses her advances. She turns against him, and convinces Fionn to outlaw Dearc Corra. Some time later, Fionn comes upon a mysterious figure in the forest:

> co n-aca Find in fer i n-úachtar in craind ⁊ lon for a gūalainn ndeis ⁊ find-lestar n-uma for a lāimh clī, osē co n-usce ⁊ hē brecc bedcach and ⁊ dam allaith fo bun in craind.

> Finn ... saw a man in the top of a tree, a blackbird on his right shoulder and in his left hand a white vessel of bronze, filled with water, in which was a skittish trout, and a stag at the foot of the tree.[7]

This mysterious figure is seen to share the water and an apple with blackbird, stag, and trout. Fionn, looking on with wonder, sucks his thumb to gain understanding of the scene before him. In a *rosc*, the identity of Dearc Corra is revealed to Fionn.[8] Following from

---

[5] Ed. from TCD MS H.3.18 (1337) by Meyer, 'Find and the Man in the Tree'.
[6] Meyer's translation represents the name of the servant as Derg Corra (MS forms: Dercc / Derc Corra mac Uí Daighre). Carey has demonstrated ('Two Notes on Names', 120–3) that the final *c* is unvoiced and that the name is best understood as Derc Corra moccu Daigre.
[7] Meyer, 'Find and the Man in the Tree', 346–7, §3.
[8] Another attempt to address this difficult language has been made by Hull, 'A Rhetoric in *Finn and the Man in the Tree*'.

Meyer's understanding of the poem, the interpretation of the text has often been shamanistic, focusing on the mysterious elements as pagan remnant. Kaarina Hollo contributes another reading, however, stressing the breaking of the apple and sharing of the water leading to enlightenment as a Christian Eucharistic image, reminding readers that this early literature, strange though it may be, is the product of monastic scriptoria.[9] An expanded account of the opening events of this tale is also extant, titled *Tucait Fhagh-bala in Fesa do Finn inso ocus Marbad Cuil Duib* ('How Finn Obtained Knowledge, and the Slaying of Cúldub').[10]

'The Quarrel between Finn and Oisín', as Kuno Meyer named it, is a comic narrative based on the folk-motif of the failure of recognition. This text may also date from the eighth century.[11] Fionn comes upon Oisín unawares in a wood; Oisín has been angry with his father and has been absent from the *fían* for a year. Fionn strikes Oisín, who does not recognise him. Most of the piece consists of a series of insults and challenges in verse exchanged between the young warrior and the grey-haired man until they recognise each other.

Scél asa mberar combad hé Find mac Cumaill Mongán ('A Story from which it is Inferred that Mongán was Finn mac Cumaill'), a relatively widely circulated anecdote preserved as part of a series of short texts about Mongán, is one of the most intriguing texts in the early literature. It is preserved in a pre-Norman copy in LU, the oldest manuscript to contain Fenian-Cycle texts.[12] In it, Mongán is threatened with satire for contradicting his poet Forgoll; they make a wager on whether Mongán can prove his position. Just before the time for Mongán to prove himself elapses, he is visited by Caoilte, who provides the evidence and who then inadvertently divulges that Mongán is Fionn, reborn. The longevity of the disguised ancient, and also of Caoilte hint at the literary development of the cycle to come. The brief text is puzz-

---

9 '"Finn and the Man in the Tree" as Verbal Icon'.

10 Ed. and trans. Meyer, 'Two Tales about Finn', 245–7, from RIA Stowe MS D iv 2; from YBL and D iv 2 by Hull, in 'Two Tales about Find', 329–33, with discussion of the age of the texts (pp. 322–3).

11 Preserved in BLL Harleian MS 5280; RIA MS 23 N 10 (967), and NLS Adv. MS 72.3.5 (Gaelic MS LXXXIII), a nineteenth-century transcript from the lost Book of Kilbride. The text is ed. and trans. by Meyer, *Fianaigecht*, 22–7.

12 Ed. and trans. by White in *Compert Mongáin and Three Other Early Mongán Tales*, 73–4 (text), 81–2 (trans.), 116–60 (notes). Previous editions and scholarship are discussed on pp. 1–4, the manuscript witnesses on pp. 5–25.

11

ling in many ways. The contents of this anecdote do not recur in the later literature, and despite the alternative accounts of the death of Fionn, there is no re-iteration of this claim for his possible survival.

The tenth century provides the first glimpse of the tragedy of the star-crossed lovers Diarmaid and Gráinne.[13] An account is given of Fionn's wooing of Gráinne that is not in agreement with the lengthy versions in later tradition. Gráinne, the daughter of high-king Cormac mac Airt, wishing to be rid of an unwanted suitor (Fionn) imposes an impossible request: a pair of every animal in Ireland, as a condition of her consent to the match. Fionn's nephew Caoilte, renowned for his swiftness, accomplishes the feat quickly and fetches the animals to Tara. By the end of the marriage feast, however, Fionn has realised that the union can never be happy and that separation is inevitable. The story, with a different frame, re-appears in a late medieval version in verse where Caoilte accomplishes the feat to free Fionn, who has been taken prisoner by Cormac after a quarrel.[14]

Two tales provide background information on the cycle. *Fotha Catha Cnucha* ('The Cause of the Battle of Cnucha') relates the tale of Fionn's father, Cumhall.[15] Like *Scél asa mberar combad hé Find mac Cumaill Mongán*, it is preserved in LU. The druid Nuadha and his wife Almha build a stronghold on the Hill of Allen named after her.[16] Their son Tadhg inherits it, and he in turn has a daughter Muirne. Cumhall, Fionn's father, abducts her after Tadhg refuses to consent to the match. Tadhg seeks justice from the high-king, Conn Céadchathach, who sends warriors after Cumhall. Aodh mac Morna slays Cumhall, losing an eye in the battle, and thus receives the name Goll ('One-eyed'). Muirne bears a posthumous son to Cumhall, whom she delivers to Bodhbhmhall the druidess, Cumhall's sister, to rear. The tale leaps forward in time to the point when the young Fionn challenges Tadhg over his father's death:

---

[13] Ed. and trans. by Meyer, 'Finn and Grainne'; ed. with German trans. by Corthals, 'Die Trennung von Find und Gráinne'. Diarmaid is also mentioned in passing in *Bruiden Átha hÍ*: Meyer, 'Two Tales about Find', 242.

[14] A number of versions of this poem survive with varying degrees of modernisation and abbreviation. The two earliest are in BDL (see Ross, *Heroic Ballads*, 40–59 [ll. 469–760]); and *DF* i, lay VII.

[15] Diplomatic edition, *LU* 101–3 (ll. 3135–219). Ed. and trans. by Hennessy, 'The Battle of Cnucha'; updated trans. in Nagy, *Wisdom of the Outlaw*, 218–21.

[16] *Almu*, modern *Almha*; the dative *Almhain* is the basis of the English form.

Cuinchis Find for Tadg na tor
i Cumall mór do marbod.
cath can chardi do can dáil
no comrac oenfir d'fagbail

Tadg uair nír tualaing catha
i n-agid na ardfhlatha.
ro fhac leis ba loor do
mar boi uli Almo.

Fionn demanded of Tadhg of the towers,
for the killing of great Cumhall,
battle without delay or hesitation;
[he demanded that he] get single combat.

Tadhg, because he could not wage battle
against the high lord,
left to him (it was sufficient for him)
all of Almha, just as it was.[17]

The text concludes with Goll making peace by payment also, leaving Fionn as the undisputed lord of Almha.

The most important information about Fionn as a character, however, is found in the fragmentary *Macgnímartha Finn*, which is generally dated to the twelfth century.[18] Deimhne, the posthumous son of Cumhall, is reared in secret by two female *féinnidhthe* in ignorance of his identity, lest Clann Mhorna destroy him. He first receives the nickname Fionn from a troop of boys whom he alone defeats at hurling. The kings of Beanntraighe and Carbraighe recognise Deimhne's parentage by his prowess at hunting and 'chess' (*fidhcheall*). In search of his uncle Criomhall, Deimhne encounters a number of adventures before he finally meets him and the remainder of the *fian* of Clann Bhaoiscne. He decides to train as a poet under Fionnéigeas (Fionn the Seer), who catches the 'salmon of knowledge', resulting not only in a poetic revela-

---

[17] Text from *LU* 102–3 (ll. 3202–9); trans. Nagy, *Wisdom of the Outlaw*, 220–1.
[18] The text is preserved in the Book of the White Earl (BLO Laud MS 610). Ed. Meyer, 'Macgnímartha Find'; trans. idem, 'The Boyish Exploits of Finn'; there is an earlier ed. and trans. by O'Donovan, 'Mac-gnimartha Finn Mac Cumaill'. More recent translations have been made available by Nagy, *Wisdom of the Outlaw*, 209–18; and by Carey in Koch and Carey, *The Celtic Heroic Age*, 183–91, §74.

tion for Fionn, but the confirmation of Fionn as Deimhne's proper name:

Frith in mbradan ocus ro herbad do Demne immorro in bradán do fuine ocus asbert an file fris cen ní don bradan do tomailt. Dobert in gilla do an bradan iar n-a fuine. 'Inar tomlis ní don bradan, a gilla?' ol in file. 'Ni to' ol in gilla, 'acht mo ordu do loisces ocus doradus im beolu iartaín'. 'Cia hainm fil ort-sa, a gilla?' ol sé. 'Demne' ol in gilla. 'Finn do ainm', ol se 'a gilla, ocus is duit tucad in bradan dia tomailt, ocus is tu in Find co fír'.

The salmon was caught, and was entrusted to Deimne to cook; and the poet told him not to eat any of it. The lad brought the salmon to him after he had cooked it. 'Did you eat any of the salmon, lad?' said the poet. 'No', said the lad; 'but I burnt my thumb and put it in my mouth after that'. 'What is your name, lad?' he said. 'Deimne', said the lad. 'Finn is your name, lad', he said, 'and it is you who were destined to eat the salmon; truly you are the fair one (*in finn*)'.[19]

Fionn suddenly demonstrates mastery of the art of poetry by composing a long and obscure chant in language substantially older than that of the prose text in which it is embedded, describing the beauty of Mayday. It begins:

Céttemain cáin ré!
rosaír cucht and:
canait luin láíd láin
día mbeith lái gái gann.

May-day, season surpassing!
Splendid is colour then.
Blackbirds sing a full lay,
If there be a slender shaft of day.[20]

---

[19] Text from Meyer, 'Macgnímartha Find', 201, §18; trans. Carey in Koch and Carey, *Celtic Heroic Age*, 188.

[20] This passage is from Meyer's limited restoration of the text in *Four Old-Irish Songs of Summer and Winter*, 8–9, §1. A diplomatic version is printed in Meyer, 'Macgnímartha Find', 201, §20. Another translation may be found in Jackson, *Studies in Early Celtic Nature Poetry*, 23–4, §25. An ambitious reconstruction of the poem, departing to a much greater extent from the manuscript readings, is Murphy, *Early Irish Lyrics*, 156–9, §52;

The remainder of the text describes hostile encounters with the *aos sídhe*. The patchwork that is the *Macgnímartha* bears testimony to the variety and vigour of Fenian tradition at the time of its composition.

The largest body of early items in this cycle is to be found in the tales and poems of the *dinnsheanchas* (older *dindsenchas*), a collection of anecdotes about the supposed origins of place-names. The *dinnsheanchas* associates *fianaigheacht* closely with particular toponyms, nearly always those of the wilderness, rather than of settlements — as is quite appropriate for bands of hunters dwelling on the borders beyond ordinary habitation. A large portion of this lore with Fenian associations portrays the institution as a violent one. Cuirreach Life ('The Curragh of Kildare') is said to derive its name from a man of that name whom Fionn slew there. Tiobra Sean-Gharmna is the well into which Fionn threw Sean-Gharman's body after killing him. Nearly any place with a name 'Ceann X' can be explained by someone, not infrequently a Fenian, coming and decapitating warrior X, leaving or placing the head there; thus Ceann Finiochair, the site of the beheading of Finiochar. It is immediately apparent to the modern reader that these tales do not provide a true explanation of these place-names, but they provide excellent documentation of their authors' attitudes to Fionn and his warriors.

There is a second class of *dinnsheanchas* poems worthy of note here, those that cite Fionn as their author; many of them have no Fenian content: the association comes in a heading such as *Finn ro chan* or *Finn cecinit* ('Fionn sang'). These attributions are inconsistent between manuscripts; many such attributions — including many of those from early and important manuscripts such as LL — were ignored altogether by Gwynn in his edition of *The Metrical Dindshenchas*. Rolf Baumgarten analyses how the early medieval etymological (Isidorean) method underlies both personal names and place-names in *fianaigheacht* in the sources beyond the canonical *dinnsheanchas*. His analysis of the tale *Bruiden Átha hÍ* demonstrates that the version of the tale presented in the *dinnsheanchas* has already degenerated, the author failing to understand the learned etymological element fully; the same fault is found elsewhere in the *dinnsheanchas* and in *AcS*.[21] Baumgarten's

Murphy's edition is strongly criticised, and a normalised text edition with far less emendation and a translation is offered by Carney in 'Three Old-Irish Accentual Poems', 30–52.

[21] Baumgarten, 'Placenames, Etymology, and *Fianaigecht*'; the discussion of Bruiden Átha hÍ is at pp. 7–17. The initial portion of Baumgarten's article

argument that the period of the greatest flourishing of such learned *fianaigheacht* was in the early medieval period has a tantalising implication: that large quantities of such written material have perished. While simple etymologising does play a role in Old and Middle Irish *fianaigheacht*, Murray explores a number of further applications of toponyms, including multiple namings and the use of places with names that bear on the plots of tales in other ways, demonstrating how toponomy plays varied roles in the early tales and poems. He concludes that the cycle 'shows the centrality of place-names, and particularly the *dinnshenchas* tradition, to both the creation and dissemination of much of this literature'.[22]

Along with the narratives and poems, there is a strong enumerative tradition within the Fenian Cycle, which did not confine itself to lists of sons or even warbands, but often digressed into lengthy passages of description. The most famous such text is *Áirem Muintire Finn* ('The Enumeration of Fionn's People'), an account of Fionn's household and retinue.[23] The passage begins with a description of the legal status of a *féinnidh* as outside the legal framework of *tuath* and clan for purposes of reprisal and honour-price. The idealised qualifications of *féinnidhthe* are then listed:

> Ní gabthái fer díb so co mbo rífili dá leabar déc na filidhechta. ní gabtha fer díb fós co nderntái latharlog mór co roiched fillidh a uathróigi. ocus no chuirthe ann é ocus a sciath les ocus fad láime do chronn chuill. ocus nónbar laech iar sin chuigi co nái sleguib leo ocus deich nimuiri atturru co ndibruigidís i nóinfecht é. ocus dá ngontai thairis sin é ní gabtai a bfianoigecht.

> Of all these again not a man was taken until he were a prime poet versed in twelve books of poesy. No man was taken till in the ground a large hole had been made (such as to reach the

---

(pp. 4–5) addresses the name Oisín; see also Ó Briain, 'Oisín's Biography', esp. 460–7 and 480–5. Arbuthnot examined an etymological undercurrent in anecdotes relating to the name of Oisín's son, 'On the Name Oscar and Two Little-known Episodes Involving the *Fían*'. For a brief account of the literary use of names and naming practices in Irish literature, see Baumgarten, 'Etymological Aetiology in Irish Tradition'.

[22] Murray, 'Place-names in the Early *Fíanaigecht* Corpus', 457.

[23] In BLL Egerton MS 1782; BLL Harleian MS 5280; and BLis. O'Grady's partial edition from Egerton 1782 in *Silva Gadelica* (i, 92–3; trans. ii, 99–101) cuts off after the narrative portion of the passage without printing the entire text as found in the manuscript. The text has been re-edited and analysed in Josephine O'Connell's unpublished thesis, '*Airem Muinntari Finn* and *Anmonna Oesa Fedma Find*: Manuscripts, Scribes, and Texts'.

fold of his belt) and he put into it with his shield and a fore-arm's length of a hazel stick. Then must nine warriors, having nine spears, with a ten furrows' width betwixt them and him, assail him and in concert let fly at him. If past that guard of his he were hurt then, he was not received into Fianship.[24]

An enumeration of the offices and men of Fionn's household follows the description of a number of similar feats. Two copies of another list of the household survive in YBL.[25] Another such reckoning, containing genealogies of some individual *féinnidhthe*, may be found among the pedigrees in the sixteenth-century leaves now bound in with the manuscript of the Book of Leinster; it has received no scholarly attention to date.[26] There are many other Fenian pedigrees, the earliest (perhaps seventh century) surviving in a poem attributed to Seanchán Toirpéist, where Fionn's descent is traced back to Nuadha Neacht, the Laighin ancestor figure.[27] Sometimes these pedigrees are interwoven with literary materials, such as that in TCD MS H.3.17 (1336), col. 846, where there is an account of the offices in the *fian*. Further genealogies can be found in the Book of Lecan fo. 193v. and YBL col. 333, where a significant number of warriors are listed. Against this background of writing exuberant Fenian lore within the semi-historical geneal-ogies, there stand only the annalistic obituaries of Fionn amid the more soberly historical sources.[28]

Among the many texts of undisputedly older origin discuss-ed above, most are found in comparatively late manuscripts with the significant exceptions of *Fotha Catha Cnucha* and *Scél asa mberar combad hé Find mac Cumaill Mongán*, both preserved (as noted above) in LU. However, in the twelfth century, one large manuscript witness, LL, provides a different kind of opportunity to see the literary development of the cycle because it preserves a corpus of different types of Fenian texts of that period together in the context of the 'Great Book' (to use James Carney's phrase) including multiple texts of the cycle, other heroic literature, and

---

[24] O'Grady, *Silva Gadelica*, ed. i, 92; trans. ii, 100.

[25] Ed. with German trans. by Stern, 'Fiannsruth'.

[26] This material, found in the later leaves bound in at the end of the manu-script, is not in Best and Bergin's diplomatic edition, nor has it been digit-ised; in addition to the original manuscript or microfilm, the text may be accessed in the transcribed facsimile of the Royal Irish Academy, *The Book of Leinster*, p. 379a. See Arbuthnot, 'Some Accretions'.

[27] Corthals, 'The Rhymeless "Leinster Poems"', 121–2.

[28] See below p. 60.

much else.[29] In the codex's opening section, containing historical and pseudo-historical material, the poem of Giolla an Choimdheadh ua Cormaic '*A Rí Ríchid, réidig dam*' ('O King of Heaven, smooth out for me') gives a series of allusions to multiple episodes involving Fionn, including his recovery of Cumhall's mysterious *corrbholg*.[30] The manuscript also contains significant *dinnsheanchas* materials with their Fenian associations, and the *Bórama*, a tale of the cattle-tribute paid by Leinster, which contains a significant episode in which Fionn and the Fenians win the Leinstermen a respite. There are further poems concerning the Fenian Cycle embedded in other kinds of texts in the manuscript, as well as marginalia, including two quatrains on the birth of Oisín. Seven independent items, however, stand out as a group.

The first of these is the poem '*Ogum i llia lia uas lecht*' ('An ogham on a flagstone, a flagstone on a grave'), a short recollection by Oisín on the battle of Gabhair, in which his son Oscar and the high-king Cairbre Lifeachair slew each other.[31] There follows a long poem '*Ligi Guill i mMaig Raigni*' ('The grave of Goll in Mag Raigne') — more than eighty quatrains — in which Fionn praises the bravery of Goll mac Morna and recites an exhaustive catalogue of his victories. This version of the text, which is substantially longer than later copies, received little attention until its recent full-length edition and study.[32]

The poem '*Óenach indiu luid in rí*' ('Today, the king went to a fair') is frequently called 'Find and the Phantoms' from the title given to its first edition by Whitley Stokes.[33] It vividly sketches

---

[29] The 'Great Book' is a type of manuscript containing a thematic compilation of history, genealogy, and literature presented as a collection designed to encompass the world of Irish antiquarian learning, and the contents of which are designed as a status symbol of the patron's (and his court's) command of and devotion to learning; see Carney, 'Literature in Irish', 690–3.

[30] Ed. and trans. by Meyer, *Fianaigecht*, 46–51.

[31] Ed. and trans. by O'Curry in O'Kearney, 'The Battle of Gabhra', 49–51; re-edited by Windisch (with a reprint of O'Curry's translation) in 'Drei Gedichte aus der Finnsage', 157–60.

[32] Ó Murchadha, *Lige Guill*. A later version of the poem, from which nearly a hundred quatrains of the list of battles has been excised, is found in *DF* (lay XLVIII, which is a re-arranged segment beginning at q. 48 of the *LL* text).

[33] *LL* ll. 29089–300; ed. and trans. by Stokes, 'Find and the Phantoms', 289–307. A new Modern Irish translation is forthcoming in Ó Síocháin, 'Translating *Find and the Phantoms* into Modern Irish'. A later version of this lay is number XIII in *DF*; a section of it is quoted in *AcS*: Stokes, 'Acallamh na Senórach', ll. 1595–618; later versions of the *Agallamh*, including *AgS*, interpolate the entire lay (cf. *AgS* i, 169–82; the poem begins on p. 173,

18

a change from colourful sport to horror. Fionn and the *fiana* attend horse-races and a feast. In high spirits, the Fenians race each other through the countryside, until they find themselves in the wilderness at dusk, asking hospitality from the only house in view. Horrible monsters appear in the house and sing a ghastly music. They are served their own horses — flayed before their eyes — for their dinner, *feóil om ar beirib carthind*, 'raw meat on rowan spits'.[34] Their treatment provokes a desperate fight against their unearthly hosts, until the hostel dissolves in mist at dawn and they find their wounds gone and horses unharmed. A prose version of this story, containing some linguistically earlier features, also exists; the two texts frequently display verbal correspondence in the scenes in the supernatural hostel, but there are additional short episodes concluding the prose version (not reflected in the lay) regarding the tensions between Fionn and Aodh (Goll), oddly leading to a prophecy of the coming of Saint Ciarán. In a number of places, the author of the poem has clearly modified his source with improved literary effect.[35] Also notable is the persona of the narrator, who identifies himself at the beginning as 'Guaire dall'. He is none other than Oisín, now elderly and blind. The account anticipates the extended recitations by Caoilte and Oisín in *AcS*. This is the oldest extant example in manuscript, and possibly the oldest text,[36] of a heroic narrative Fenian lay or ballad, a form that later came to dominate the literature. Its introduction is a major turning point as there is no sign of narrative poetry in Old Irish at all. The first heroic narrative verse in Irish, which does not long precede the text of 'Find and the Phantoms', is embedded in the Ulster-Cycle prosimetric tale, *Siaburcharpat Con Culaind* ('Cú Chulainn's Ghostly Chariot'), the earliest copy of which is preserved in LU.[37] This provides a model for both the heroic poetry and the setting of engagement by Christian and royal

---

following a précis in prose). There is further analysis of these three versions in Van Kranenburg, '"Oenach indiu luid in rí"'.

[34] *LL* l. 29247.

[35] The prose text is preserved in Leiden, Universiteit Bibliotheken, Isaac Vossii cod. lat. quart. No. 7 ('The Leyden Irish MS'). Ed. with French translation by Stern, 'Le Manuscrit Irlandais de Leide'.

[36] Dated to the eleventh century by Meyer, *Fianaigecht*, p. xxv, §xxxi.

[37] *LU* ll. 9220–548; ed. and trans. by O'Beirne Crowe 'Siabur-charpat Con Culaind'. O'Beirne Crowe's translation contains numerous inaccuracies, and a modern edition is much to be desired. The thesis of Feargal Ó Béarra, 'A Critical Edition of Siaburcharpat Con Culaind', will remedy this deficiency: publication of this work is forthcoming as *Siaburcharpat Con Culainn*.

figures with a revivified or surviving figure from the heroic past, which is the template for much subsequent Fenian literature.

Another narrative poem, '*Dám thrír táncatar ille*' ('A company of three men came here'), usually known as 'The Hound of Iruaith', tells of a quarrel between Fionn and a group of three invaders with a man-slaying hound. Fionn and the Fenians pursue the attackers in an adventure in the East, ending with a lament for the men lost in the quest.[38] There are also two short laments: '*Tuilsitir mo derca suain*' ('My eyes reposed in sleep') attributed to the aged Oisín and '*Bec innocht lúth mo dá lua*' ('Small tonight the vigour of my heels'), put into the mouth of Caoilte.[39] Finally, LL preserves part of a short tale concerning Fionn sending Mac Leasc ('Lazy lad'), his serving boy, for water. Mac Leasc asserts that he will not go out into the severe weather, and recites a lyric on wintry chill. In another copy of this text preserved in BLO Rawlinson MS B. 502, Fionn responds with a longer lyric on fine weather before proceeding to cure Mac Leasc of his laziness:

> Atberat som tra ropo écen dó-som techt do íarair ind usci 7 rocengalt Find lomnocht co matain do Choirthi Chuilt, co nád búi i féin Find fer bad áiniu 7 bad escaidiu ó sain 'mach.

> They say, however, that he had perforce to go to seek the water, and Finn bound him stark naked to Colt's standing-stone till the morning, so that henceforth no one in the warband of Finn was quicker and more untiring.[40]

In '*Bec innocht lúth mo dá lua*', reference is made to Saint Patrick: *naco toracht in Talcend*, 'before the coming of the Adzehead'. Although the addressee of these verses is unnamed, the likeliest explanation is that they fit within the framework of recitation of poems by Oisín and Caoilte to Saint Patrick that dominates the later literature. In these, one sees nearly all the aspects prominent in Fenian verse in the later medieval and Early Modern periods: the lament of the ancients; a praise-poem; a *bruidhean* (a hostile Otherworld encounter) told at length in narrative verse; a

---

[38] Ed. with German translation by Stern, 'Eine ossianische Ballade aus dem XII. Jahrhundert'; the anonymous review of the *Festschrift* in *Zeitschrift für celtische Philologie* 3, 432–4, prints the text from BLis.

[39] The former is edited by Windisch in 'Drei Gedichte aus der Finnsage', 161–4; the latter by Meyer, 'Cáilte Cecinit. Book of Leinster, p. 208a'.

[40] Ed. and trans. by Meyer, *Four Old-Irish Songs of Summer and Winter*, 16–23, at 22–3.

conflict with an invader; two nature lyrics; and sundry short learned items. By the twelfth century, not only were all the major elements of the Fenian Cycle present, but they had been assembled to the extent that such a collection could be found within the covers of a single codex.

3. *Agallamh na Seanórach*
'The Colloquy of the Ancients'

When scholars speak of *Acallam na Senórach* using the Middle
Irish spelling, it is usually the earliest recension to which they
refer.[1] There are four major families of texts of the *Agallamh*
tradition, and so much reworking of the prose sections (never
mind more substantial addition and substitution of episodes) that
there is hardly a manuscript that agrees with another. *AcS* is the
product of a transitional point in the literary history of the cycle
and a milestone in its development. Formerly estimated to stand at
the end of the twelfth century, Nuner suggested a date of 1200–25
on linguistic grounds,[2] and recent studies based on content have
supported these dates. Dooley's exploration of the immediate purpose of the text as a political example for Cathal Croibhdhearg,
king of Connaught (r. 1190–1200; 1202–24), has led to further
modifications by Anne Connon, who propounds that the text was
composed in the monastery of Roscommon, by the scholar-abbot
Tiobraide Ó Briain (†1232) (or alternatively the magister of the
school, Maol Peadair Ó Cormacáin), c. 1224–5 at the opening of
the reign of Cathal's son and successor Aodh.[3] Connon's theory
integrates well with Annie Donahue's exposition of the composition's use as 'a medieval instruction manual for canon marriage';[4]
it also resonates with Ní Mhaonaigh's observation, drawn from
AcS alongside other contemporary Irish texts, that 'vernacular
material is influenced by a range of European trends emanating
from one of the defining movements of the period, religious
reform'.[5]

    The earliest recension is preserved in five manuscripts,
three of them dated to the fifteenth century.[6] The text is incom-

---

[1] In this essay, the abbreviations *AcS* and *AgS* are used for the particular
versions specified, but *Agallamh* (*na Seanórach*) in Classical spelling will
be written when the reference is to the more extended tradition, including
other, later versions. For editions and translations of *AcS*, see p. 6, n. 24.

[2] See Nuner, 'The Verbal System of the *Agallamh na Senórach*'.

[3] Dooley, 'The Date and Purpose of *Acallam na Senórach*'; Connon, 'The
Roscommon *Locus* of *Acallam na Senórach*'.

[4] Donahue, 'The *Acallam na Senórach*: A Medieval Instruction Manual', 214.

[5] Ní Mhaonaigh, 'Pagans and Holy Men: Literary Manifestations of Twelfth-
century Reform', 161.

[6] The three early witnesses are BLO Rawlinson MS B. 487; The Book of the
White Earl (BLO Laud MS 610); and BLis. A fourth witness is UCD
Archives, Franciscan MS A4, a sixteenth-century copy which diverges from

plete in all witnesses; nevertheless, it is still the longest extant text in medieval Irish. Although these manuscripts contain broadly the same version of the same tale, they have a wide variety of variants in phrasing and detail in virtually every line. Furthermore, there is re-ordering of episodes and a few sections that are not held in common among all witnesses. The stemma of the manuscripts has not been satisfactorily established to date, and new editions are required if the present level of scholarly activity is to be sustained.

Stokes' text, which is the most used, is syncretistic, jumping back and forth from basing its text on BLO Laud MS 610 (The Book of the White Earl) to BLis., adding passages and even episodes from the other manuscripts when they are longer and more developed than in another source, or when they are not found in his chosen witness. His idea of the original is based on the idea of loss (rather than accretion) as the operative principle, piecing nearly everything together into the longest possible text, presumably on the grounds of a desire for completeness; yet other unquestionably original passages, the locations of which are variable in the manuscripts, are relegated to appendices. From the edition, it is not possible to follow through the text of any manuscript. Furthermore, Thanisch has recently demonstrated that Stokes' treatment of the manuscript materials that he is following at any point can be shockingly uneven, with some omission of manuscript headings, glosses, and marginalia.[7] O'Grady's edition, presenting the text of BLis., is faithful to the content of that manuscript's version; nevertheless, it fails to meet scholars' needs because his nineteenth-century attempt at orthographical standardisation misses — and normalises away — features of Middle Irish, especially in the verse. O'Grady, for example, was ignorant of the distinction between absolute and conjunct verbal forms that did not survive in the modern language.[8] Future study of the structure of *AcS* must untangle the problems of the various manuscript witnesses rather than attempting to construct a single critical text. At present, scholarship must frequently return to the manuscripts

---

the others to a greater extent; the fifth witness, Franciscan MS A20a, which is bound with DF, contains a version of the text copied from A4. For a discussion of the recensions and the manuscripts, see Ó Muraíle, 'Agallamh na Seanórach', in addition to the prefaces to the editions listed above on p. 6, n. 24.

[7] Thanisch, 'What the Butlers Saw'.

[8] For further discussion of the early editors and their scholarly approaches to editing, see Parsons, 'Whitley Stokes, Standish Hayes O'Grady, and *Acallam na Senórach*'.

when attempting literary analysis, highlighting once more the need for new editions.

AcS relates the journeys of the aged Caoilte and Oisín in prosimetrum form. As the text opens, they part, and Caoilte is converted and accepted into the retinue of Saint Patrick. They travel a circuit of Ireland, during which Caoilte tells Patrick the *dinnsheanchas* of the places through which they pass, identifying graves, battlefields, and monuments; and, as occasions on the journey suggest appropriate moments, he recites lore on subjects such as the names of the hounds of the *fian*, the description of their drinking horns, and also provides learned notes on their customs. Oisín, meanwhile, attaches himself in a similar lore-giving role to the king of Tara. The ancients are re-united at the royal fair after a year, then make a second circuit with Saint Patrick. The tale breaks off in its epilogue, in which Caoilte and Oisín have returned to Tara, where their retinue of aged Fenians die, and the last pair are left narrating the history of the Lia Fáil, or Stone of Destiny. It may be assumed, with the support of later versions of the text, that the deaths of the converted ancients would follow quite shortly thereafter and bring the work to its natural conclusion. The surviving portion of the work is therefore nearly complete.[9] *AcS* is mostly episodic, comprised of short tales and poems recited within the prose frame-tale of Saint Patrick's missionary journeys. On grounds of style, there is a scholarly consensus that that many of the episodes originated as independent *laoithe*, the plots of which have been summarised in a prose retelling. This could account for the few quatrains accompanying many of them, which may have been retained from a verse original as an ornament to the *Acallam*. On the other hand, other short poems, especially single-quatrain items, seem to have been composed for their setting in *AcS*. In so long a work with so many constituent materials, there is substantial disagreement about the extent to which the in-tales have been integrated and adapted for their settings. The question is speculative in many instances because only a small proportion of *AcS*'s literary sources are extant.[10] The only surviving Fenian lays for which the manuscript witnesses antedate the composition of *AcS* are those in LL; nevertheless, a number of other collections — including LUM and DF — contain poems with linguistic features characteristic of the

---

[9] *Pace* Nagy, who suggests the possibility that 'the *Acallam* never had an ending' ('Life in the Fast Lane', 131).

[10] Dooley and Roe, *Tales of the Elders*, p. xvii; Parsons, '*Acallam na Senórach* as Prosimetrum'; Carney, 'Two Poems from *Acallam na Senórach*'.

Middle Irish period, which suggest that they originate centuries earlier than the surviving copies. Since an early thirteenth-century date is now generally accepted for *AcS*, which is later than a number of Fenian lays that incorporate Patrician-Fenian dialogue, it is clear that this premise cannot be original to *AcS*. The state of the evidence, however, makes exact evaluation of a timescale impossible.[11]

As a composition, *AcS* weaves together diverse strands of *fianaigheacht* on a grand scale with a sophisticated structure. Geraldine Parsons detects two distinct thematic series of in-tales in *AcS*, one relating to Fionn's precocious monotheism and prophecies, the other outlining the relations between Clann Bhaoiscne and Clann Mhorna. These series both develop and refer to the context of the frame story's own progression: though *AcS* on its surface follows a simple geographical circuit, its construction is not unsophisticated.[12] Dooley stresses the didactic element, in which episodes suggest commentary on the political situation of early thirteenth-century Connaught.[13] Whatever their origins or new uses, the contents of the in-tales are quite in keeping with the earlier literature, despite a shift to a more celebratory tone. In one of the most famous passages of the work, the angels signal their approval of Fenian lore to Saint Patrick. As he sees Caoilte and his men approach, he blesses them, and a host of demons depart from them at once. Caoilte begins to describe the days of his prime to Patrick, and the saint approves. The next morning, he is given instructions by the angels:

'A anum, a naeimchléirigh!' ar siat, 'ní mó iná trian a scél innisit na senlaeich út ar dáigh dermait ⁊ dichuimhne. Ocus scríbhthar letsa i támlorguibh filed ⁊ i mbriat[h]raibh ollaman, ór budh gairdiugudh do dronguibh ⁊ do degdáinibh deridh aimsire éisdecht frisna scéluib sin'.

'Dear holy cleric', they said, 'these old warriors tell you no more than a third of their stories because their memories are faulty. Have these stories written down on poets' tablets in

---

[11] See Parsons, Review of Carey (ed.), *Duanaire Finn: Reassessments*.

[12] Parsons, 'The Structure of *Acallam na Senórach*'; Nagy, 'Compositional Concerns in the *Acallam na Senórach*'. The careful construction is not only evident in the frame's structure, but carries down to the smaller portions of the itinerary and the items linked with them, as Connon demonstrated through a Mayo case study in 'Plotting *Acallam na Senórach*'.

[13] Dooley, 'The Date and Purpose of *Acallam na Senórach*'.

refined language, so that the hearing of them will provide entertainment for the lords and commons of later times'.[14]

The ancients' tales are moderated through Saint Patrick and preserved; the Fenians are working under a new authority in this text.[15] Indeed, the very structure of the frame-tale parallels Patrick's circuits in the Tripartite Life, and *AcS* borrows narrative devices from the hagiographical tradition.[16] In the *Acallam*, ecclesiastical opprobrium has been explicitly lifted from *fianaigheacht* and, in return, the Fenian warriors have accepted Christianity through baptism;[17] these themes have already been foreshadowed in *Siaburcharpat Con Culaind* and in some of the earlier Fenian lays. As in *Tochmarc Ailbe* and *Macgnímartha Finn*, cultivation of the link to the high-kingship — itself seen with the rosy glow of nostalgia in the aftermath of the Norman conquest — serves to strengthen the idea of the *fian* as a protective unit rather than a cause of gratuitous violence; Nagy describes *AcS* as a 'tri-cycle' work, arching between *fianaigheacht*, the Cycles of the Kings, and Patrician hagiography.[18] Dooley observes that the purified, baptised Caoilte's actions serve as a mediator of the tradition, stressing the continuity of memory and music from an earlier age into Christian Ireland. *AcS* uses an Irish structure — the prosimetrum saga — and a native style; yet, the integration of these themes to reclaim the heroic past is paralleled in European literature of the period, such as the lays of Marie de France.[19] Nagy also explores the role of Caoilte as cultural mediator, with

---

[14] Text from Stokes, '*Acallamh na Senórach*', ll. 297–302 (equivalent to O'Grady, *Silva Gadelica*, i, 101); trans. Dooley and Roe, *Tales of the Elders*, 12.

[15] The theme of memory, writing, and preservation is examined by Schlüter, 'For the Entertainment of Lords and Commons'; see also Nagy, 'Oral Tradition in the *Acallam na Senórach*'.

[16] Dooley, 'The Deployment of Some Hagiographical Sources'. The other side of the dialogue, the acceptance of the ancient cultural inheritance by the Church, which here entails the creation of a fictional character of Saint Patrick, is stressed by Roe, 'The *Acallam*: The Church's Eventual Acceptance'; see also Roe, '*Acallam na Senórach*: The Confluence of Lay and Clerical Oral Traditions'.

[17] See Ní Mhaonaigh, 'Pagans and Holy Men', 151–5.

[18] Nagy, '*Acallam na Senórach*: A Tri-cycle'. The thematic unity of presentation of tales stressing the nobility and morality of the *fiana*, narrated by the benign figure of Caoilte, to a mixed internal audience of clergy and secular lords and to the external audience of the reader is explored in idem, 'Keeping the *Acallam* Together'.

[19] See discussion in Dooley, 'The European Context of *Acallam na Senórach*'.

his dealings and bargainings with Patrick echoing the engagement between Ireland and the wider European world at the time of the text's composition.[20] The path has been cleared for Fionn to take on the mantle of a 'national hero', stretching across history, legend, and literature, as Gerard Murphy recognised.[21]

AcS is a work on a grand scale. Its prosimetric procession physically encompasses most of Ireland, and it brings the Fenian survivors into direct contact with Ireland's patron saint and major political powerhouses. It tells of many battles and relates many tales. The work, which is by far the longest piece of medieval Irish literature to survive, exceeds all others in scope; yet, it does not dominate the Fenian Cycle. When one considers the Ulster Cycle, its many narratives build towards its greatest tale, *Táin Bó Cuailgne*.[22] In contrast, even if Saint Patrick's blessing is not a minor gift, the *féinnidhthe* do not strive towards the *Acallam*'s events as a climax. Rather, they have already fulfilled their destiny, having lived through internal tensions within the *fian* and changing and difficult relationships with high-kings. Under the leadership of Fionn and with the strength of his men, they have protected Ireland from invaders and internal threats, many of them Otherworldly, until the conclusion of their heroic age. Many of them have already died in great battles — which were fought long before the narrative time of *AcS*; the few remnants have grown old. If the understanding of *fianaigheacht* as a literary cycle is rooted in the heroic biography of Fionn and heroic members of his *fian* and family, *AcS* presents the places of the Fenian dead, the burial mounds of defeated enemies, and their battles as a graveside reflection and commemoration of past events. This is integrated into the frame narrative's present, the early Christian 'Age of Saints', incorporating moral lessons intended for the author's own time in the thirteenth century: it does not tell the chief biographical story — or even the culminating battles in the history of the *fian* — but rather presumes prior knowledge of these events, reflecting the immanent nature of *fianaigheacht*.[23] In this way, *AcS* is a masterpiece of composition, but it is not the summit or focal point of Fenian literature in the way that *Táin Bó Cuailnge* is for the Ulster Cycle. On the other hand, recent scholarship is demon-

---

[20] 'Some Strands and Strains in *Acallam na Senórach*'.

[21] *DF* iii, p. lxxxvi.

[22] Among numerous versions, the most cited editions and translations are O'Rahilly, *Táin Bó Cúalnge from the Book of Leinster*; eadem, *Táin Bó Cúailnge: Recension 1*; and the literary translation by Kinsella, *The Táin*.

[23] For the terminology, see references on p. 5, n. 18.

strating that its contents and structure are even richer than had previously been thought.

AcS nevertheless marks the highest point in the development of the literature and is the first work to rejoice in Fenian heroics. It is also a high point in the learned aspects of the Fenian Cycle that throve when *dinnsheanchas* and etymology dominated *fianaigheacht* in the pre-Noman period. Though a number of the lays do celebrate learned aspects of the tradition, the narrative strand in them comes to overwhelm other aspects as the literature evolves. Even as early as *AcS*, chronological difficulties such as the anachronism of Lochlannaigh (Vikings) and failure to observe accepted regnal dates for Irish kings may hint at a decline in or manipulation of the learned element; John Carey interprets the conflation as meaningful, 'identifying the native supernatural as a whole ... as being in some sense another "time"', and presenting a constructive engagement between the times of the *fiana*, the *síodh*, the Patrician mission, and the Christian present of the narrator. Nevertheless, the recognition that there is deliberate anachronism does not in itself provide a full key for interpretation of its application.[24] Parsons draws further attention to the narrator's account, which is not simply presented as later than the Patrician dialogue, but also has independent knowledge of the past and even a prophetic dimension.[25] Ó Cadhla explores the universe portrayed from another angle, as an ethnographical compendium of the heroic world and its members — worldly or not — investigated through the ongoing 'questionnaire' put to Caoilte.[26]

The scholarly aspects of the toponymic strand in the cycle decline over time in the literature. Although a number of places in the canonical *dinnsheanchas* are now unidentifiable, the locations were clearly real places. In *AcS*, a much larger proportion is unidentifiable, despite the fact that the text is more recent. In later Fenian tradition, the trend accelerates, so that apart from a few well-known places such as Eas Ruaidh (Assaroe, Co. Donegal), Teamhair (Tara, Co. Meath), and Almha (The Hill of Allen, Co. Kildare), the 'place-names' frequently cease to document the landscape; they may actually be creations used to augment the story.[27] The geographical progression of the journey around Ire-

---

[24] See Carey, '*Acallam na Senórach*: A Conversation between Worlds', 83.

[25] Parsons, 'The Narrative Voice in *Acallam na Senórach*'.

[26] 'Approaching the *Acallam* as Ethnography', 139–43.

[27] See Ó Coileáin, 'Place and Placename in *Fianaigheacht*'. Meek describes a not unrelated phenomenon of sets of toponyms in Fenian literature moving and being applied to multiple locations in both Ireland and Scotland in

land taken by Caoilte and Saint Patrick in *AcS* is certainly quite clear. Nevertheless, a significant portion of the places named cannot be reconciled with any known locations along their routes. It is unclear whether items of *dinnsheanchas* have been invented, or older items relocated to places disconnected from their original geography. However these issues are addressed and possibly resolved, it is clear that learned detail has lost its position at the pinnacle of *fianaigheacht*.

The second recension, generally known as the *Agallamh Bheag* ('The Little Colloquy') is preserved in BLis. and in late copies made from that manuscript. Despite being discussed in scholarship under the medievalised name *Acallam Bec*, there is no manuscript authority for any form of this title, which is probably the coinage of the nineteenth-century scholar William Hennessy.[28] The *Agallamh Bheag* conflates the unwieldy double circuit of Ireland undertaken in the first recension into one to create a much shorter text, approximately a seventh of the original in length; nevertheless, it contains some additional poetry.[29] Its creator was moving away from an organisation that functioned as a mnemonic for the systematic recall of a large body of *dinnsheanchas* and other similar anecdota. Rather, it appears that his interest was primarily in narrative. No full text of the *Agallamh Bheag* has been published.[30] Several scholars have nevertheless ventured to give their opinions on its date: Dooley and Roe say that it is 'probably to be dated a little later' than the first recension, presumably in the thirteenth century; this is in concord with the

---

'Place-names and Literature: Evidence from the Gaelic Ballads'; Ó Coileáin documents the same phenomenon in 'The Setting of *Géisid Cúan*'. The basic existence, however, of a substantial portion of the place-names in *AcS* is established by Ó Muraíle, 'Agallamh na Seanórach', 120–4, and by the local case study in Connon, 'Plotting *Acallam na Senórach*'. There is a diachronic discussion of this issue in Murray, 'The Treatment of Place-names in the Early Fíanaigecht Corpus'.

[28] *AgS* i, pp. xv–xvi.

[29] The contents of this *Agallamh* are described by Kühns, 'Some Observations on the *Acallam Bec*', and contextualised by Ó Macháin, 'Aonghus Ó Callanáin, Leabhar Leasa Móir agus an Agallamh Bheag'.

[30] Hyde began a serialised edition with a Modern Irish translation, 'An Agallamh Bheag', but no further instalments were forthcoming; the published text extends to approximately a third of the full work. This portion has also been translated into English by Pennington, 'The Little Colloquy'. Kühns has prepared a text and translation in her M.Phil. thesis, 'An Edition and Translation of the *Agallamh Bheag*', which remains unpublished.

earlier observations of Nessa Ní Shéaghdha.[31]
From this second *Agallamh*, a third recension was extracted.
Virtually the entire text of the second recension was taken as the
core for expansion on a grand scale.[32] This third recension is an
Early Modern text, *AgS*, probably of the fifteenth century, that
survives in the late seventeenth-century RIA MS 24 P 5 (93), and
a nineteenth-century copy of the same, RIA MS 23 L 22 (106)
alongside a few fragments and excerpts.[33] The unique text makes
substantial changes to the *Agallamh Bheag* on which a significant
portion of it is directly and closely based, but also returns to the
longer *AcS* as the source for additional sections.[34] Oisín has replaced Caoilte, who has become a secondary figure; this change is
entirely in keeping with a similar tendency in the Fenian lays of
the same period. Numerous episodes are added, most of which
unfold in parallel prose and verse versions. It is apparent from the
language of the poems that much of the prose of *AgS* has been
composed around earlier lays.[35] Unlike the earlier recensions, this
text incorporates substantial heroic poems — a number of which
approach a hundred and fifty quatrains each — making it much
longer than even the first recension with more than 100,000
words, and nearly a third of it in verse.[36] Some of the lays,[37] such
as '*Síthiol Chaoilte*' ('Caoilte's Dipper') contain linguistic forms
substantially earlier than the prose text's; or, like '*Oidheadha na*

---

[31] Dooley and Roe, *Tales*, p. xxxi; *AgS* i, p. xix.

[32] See Kühns, 'Some Observations on the *Acallam Bec*', 137–8.

[33] Ní Shéaghdha (*AgS* i, pp. xxii–iv) identified the manuscript hand as that of
Pádraig Mac Óghannáin, an Ulster scribe active *c*. 1680–1700. A discussion
of the version in English can be found in Hyde, 'The Reeves Manuscript of
Agallamh na Senórach', which has given rise to the name 'The Reeves
Agallamh'. Ó Muraíle, however, called this version *An tAgallamh Déanach*
('The Late Colloquy') in '*Agallamh na Senórach*', and he named the modern
fourth recension *An Nua-Agallamh* ('The New Colloquy').

[34] Flahive, 'Revisiting the Reeves *Agallamh*', 166–7. See also the discussions
in Hyde, 'The Reeves Manuscript of *Agallamh na Senórach*'. The headers
in Ní Shéaghdha's edition of *AgS* cross-reference parallel passages between
AgS, *AcS*, and the *Agallamh Bheag*.

[35] Flahive, 'Revisiting the Reeves *Agallamh*', 167–83. A number of cases in
which the prose writer misunderstood the text of the poems can be found in
the text, providing further evidence of the method of compilation. One
example is in '*Síthiol Chaoilte*', where the prose redactor misread *linibh* as
léinibh. He then proceeded to describe the tunics (correctly rows of people)
using the synonym *sgúird* (ibid., 181).

[36] Ó Muraíle, '*Agallamh na Senórach*', 104.

[37] Indices to the first lines of all poems in the *Agallamh* are given in *AgS* iii,
256–61.

Féine' ('Violent Deaths of the Fian'), have learned subjects rare in Fenian material originating after the thirteenth century. Episodes such as *'Oisín agus an Chorr'* ('Oisín and the Crane') preserve legendary material of undoubted antiquity.[38] The inclusion of long narratives that are more digression than description of the history of a place, in addition to a prose style much more florid than the earlier versions of the *Agallamh*, provide evidence that new literary tastes — also evident in the evolving form of the romance, discussed in Chapter Five — are central to *AgS*.

The last group of versions, Ó Muraíle's *Nua-Agallamh*, is also Early Modern, surviving in a large number of manuscripts, postdating 1700 and generally of Munster origin. No text of this family has ever been edited or translated.[39] The language of the text has been modified significantly; succeeding generations of copyists individually modernised, cut, and interpolated even more as the taste of the scribes or patrons warranted: long before this point in its evolution, it would be fair to describe the *Agallamh* more as a genre than a text.[40]

---

[38] See Ross, 'Esus et les "Trois Grues"'.

[39] For further description of this version, see Ní Mhurchú, 'An tAgallamh Nua'.

[40] For an account of how scribes engaged with and rewrote literary texts in the Middle Irish period, with reference to the compilation of *AcS*, see Murray, 'The Reworking of Old Irish Narrative Texts'. Although the essay concludes its focus with the Middle Irish period, the model provided by Murray is a starting point for the exploration of further developments in the Early Modern era.

4. Fenian Lays

Although the form certainly came to maturity in the Middle Irish era, the Early Modern period witnessed the rise to literary prominence of the *laoithe fianaigheachta*, or Fenian lays; also called Fenian or Ossianic ballads. Strictly speaking, these terms refer to the narrative poems of the heroic deeds of the *fiana*, with each of these usually providing an account of a single adventure or event. In time, the phrase 'Fenian lay' broadened to include the lyrics and laments in the cycle, which usually employed the same verse types, becoming a broader term for Fenian verse, as opposed to prose tales and romances. In substance, the lays do not differ materially from the kinds of poems preserved in LL; for example, the type of heroic metrical narrative represented by 'Find and the Phantoms' became especially prominent in later centuries. The conventions were simple and inclusive. Any of the usual syllabic metres of the bardic schools could be employed, but the vast majority of poems favoured quatrains of *deibhidhe* and *rannaigheacht*; their heptasyllabic lines provided flexibility for sustained narration. The standards of *óglachas* were applied rather than the stricter *dán díreach* of bardic poetry for the same reason; the extent of additional ornamentation varies significantly. Although Middle Irish and Classical literary forms that were archaic in ordinary Early Modern Irish (such as older verbal forms, the inflected accusative, or infixed pronouns) were used sparingly for metrical convenience or to invoke the language of earlier heroic tales, the tendency of the lays, even for those originating in the Middle Irish period, was towards a vigorously straightforward composition rather than a refined and esoteric one. This does not necessarily mean that lays were composed by lesser poets, but it implies that this poetry served a different social function from formal bardic elegies. Some of the lyrics contain only a few stanzas, but generally the poems are longer, perhaps limited in length to what could be recited in a single performance; most complete narrative lays are between twenty and fifty quatrains, although a small number of poems are significantly longer, extending to as many as a hundred-and-fifty quatrains. Each poem usually narrates an adventure, though there are not infrequently in-tales related by the characters. Many arrange their events in a number of contrasting scenes. The surviving ancients, Oisín or Caoilte, narrate most of the poems, which they address to Saint

Patrick;[1] this convention can be presented explicitly through a framing dialogue, but it is equally as often implicit.

The manuscript tradition for Fenian lays has been frequently dismissed as rather sparse until the eighteenth century, but this is only true if the hundreds of manuscripts containing groups of dozens of lays that appear from 1750–1850 are taken as normative; it does not stand in absolute terms. Among items preserved in pre-eighteenth-century manuscripts are: narrative poems incorporated in later versions of the *Agallamh*; a number of verse prophecies attributed to Fionn on the end of the kingship of Tara, or predicting the overthrow of the English;[2] a few scattered lyrics, such as Oisín's lament on aging, '*Ro loiscit na láma-sa*' ('These hands have been withered');[3] and two large manuscripts, DF and BDL. In addition, significant amounts of heroic ballads, often in groups of twos or threes, are to be found in a number of manuscripts. Flanking the Fenian prophecies in BLO Rawlinson MS B. 514 is a poem, '*A Oisín an raide rinn*' ('Oisín, can you tell us?'),[4] a rare example of a lay (rather than a prophecy or lament) in the persona of Fionn himself. A solitary poem in the Book of the White Earl (BLO Laud MS 610), '*Ochtur táncamar anuas*' ('As an octet we descended'), describes the conversion of the ancients to Christianity.[5] Even the most perfunctory glances through the manuscript catalogues of Trinity College Dublin, the National Library of Ireland, the Royal Irish Academy, the British Library, or any major institution with even a handful of pre-eighteenth-century Gaelic literary manuscripts will likely yield up older versions of lays, published from much later witnesses only, that

---

[1] Lyrics and prophecies are not infrequently attributed to other personae, especially Fionn and Fearghus File, in which cases there is no reference to Saint Patrick.

[2] E.g. the poem '*A ben labhrus rium an laoch*' ('O woman that speaks to me the warrior'), the earliest copy of which is BLO Rawlinson MS B. 514, fo. 7r. (sixteenth century); ed. O'Keeffe, 'A Prophecy of Find'. A later copy is edited in *DF* i, 85; trans. i, 198–9; commentary iii, 72–5. Unique to Rawlinson B. 514 is another prophecy, '*Úathad mé a Temraig a-nocht*' ('Lonely am I in Tara tonight'), published by O'Keeffe as 'A Prophecy on the High-Kingship of Ireland'; a new edition with English translation has been published by Ó Muirigh, 'Fionn i nDiaidh na Ríthe'.

[3] In RIA Stowe MS D iv 2 (fifteenth century); ed. and trans. Murphy, *Early Irish Lyrics*, 166–7, §57.

[4] The DF copy of this poem has been edited and translated in *DF* ii, 154–67. A much later copy of this poem is found in TCD MS H.1.15 (1289), sometimes known as Tadhg Ó Neachtain's (or O'Noughton's) Miscellany.

[5] Ed. Stern, 'Die Bekehrung der Fianna'.

scholarship has not yet treated beyond recording their incipits. Therefore, the groundwork for a description of the high medieval and Early Modern Fenian lay has not yet been undertaken, and the full extent of the corpus remains undefined.

The earliest substantial post-Norman collection of learned medieval narrative lays is found within LUM, written in the late fourteenth century. The final section of this manuscript contains a number of lays and (pseudo-)historical poems (though only three of them belong to the Fenian Cycle); many of these poems exceed a hundred quatrains in length. Two Fenian lays, 'Uchán a sciath mo rígh réigh' ('Alas, o shield of my rightful king') and 'A chloidhimh chléirchín in chluig' ('Sword of the bell-ringing clerkling'), have a significant place in the literary development of the cycle.[6] In each, Oisín narrates the history of an object. The first of these poems describes a shield created by Manannán after the Battle of Magh Tuireadh from the wood of a hazel stained with blood from the head of Balor. The shield is traced through various owners, until it reaches Cumhall, Fionn's father, then Fionn himself. A list of victories in which Fionn wielded it then follows, ending with Oisín's lament that the ruined shield is beyond use, fit only to burn. The second lay describes Oscar's sword. This poem is more ambitious in its extent: in Oisín's recitation, the sword passes though multiple heroic cycles from the beginning of the world. It was the sword of Saturn, Jupiter, the kings of Troy, Hercules, Priam, Hector, Aeneas, Caesar, Cú Chulainn (a rather satirical and light-hearted episode), Fearghus, and Fionn himself, before he gave it to Oscar. At the close of the poem, the sword has come into the possession of a cleric, causing Oisín to lament the downfall of the heroic age and its replacement by the Christian one. These two poems also appear in Duanaire Finn, and Gerard Murphy, working only from that manuscript, declared these poems to be most likely of the mid-twelfth and thirteenth centuries respectively.[7] The third lay, in the persona of Caoilte, 'Cnucha cnoc os cionn Life' ('Cnucha, a hill overlooking the Liffey'), presents

---

[6] The former is ed. by Flahive, 'The Shield of Fionn'; an edition of the latter is in preparation by the same author. Ed. and trans. from DF only by MacNeill in DF i, where he named them 'The Shield of Fionn' and 'The Sword of Oscar'.

[7] DF iii, 34, 43–4. Murphy stated that no other copy of either text had been found; he was unaware of the existence of the LUM versions. For the date of 'Uchán a sciath mo rígh réigh' (based on both manuscripts), which agrees with that proposed by Murphy, see Flahive, 'The Shield of Fionn', 158–9.

an extended and reworked version of the *dinnsheanchas* of Cnucha with a Fenian apologue at the end.[8]

Scholarship has not yet fully addressed the significance of this group of lays in LUM; and, although versions of these texts have been published, only one utilises this important witness.[9] These three texts are very significant: unlike most earlier Irish verse relating to the heroic literary cycles, each of these poems presents its lore as part of a narrative in-tale, rather than simply versifying the information in isolation, as happens in *AcS*. These poems, along with several similar lays in Duanaire Finn, embody the transition from the two verse traditions of *seanchas* and lyric to purely narrative heroic verse. The LUM texts also provide additional warrant for the antiquity of similarly structured items found only in DF, a seventeenth-century manuscript containing a large number of unique lays, many of which contain hints of much earlier composition despite uneven scribal modernisation.

The exiled Antrim nobleman Captain Somhairle Mac Domhnaill commissioned the compilation of Duanaire Finn in Louvain in 1626–7; it is fitting that one of the books associated with this colourful noble exile should be a collection of *fianaigheacht*. Mac Domhnaill had been part of the MacDonald Rebellion in Scotland and of the Ulster Plot of 1615; he was an outlaw, a pirate, and finally a mercenary soldier for the Spanish Crown.[10] DF is closely affiliated with the College of Saint Anthony in Louvain, the intellectual powerhouse of seventeenth-century Irish scholarship that sponsored the Four Masters and collected the Lives of the saints for *Acta Sanctorum Hiberniae*.[11] Whether this manuscript was intended from the beginning for the historical programme undertaken by the college's scholars, or was a person-

---

[8] This version, quite different from the one edited by Gwynn in *The Metrical Dindshenchas*, has not been printed from this manuscript, though similarly expanded versions have been edited from later ones: see those in BLis. (with variants from RIA MS 23 O 39 [83]), ed. Power, 'Cnucha Cnoc os Cionn Life'; and RIA MS 24 P 5 (93), ed. *AgS* iii, 169–80.

[9] Flahive, 'The Shield of Fionn'; see also idem, '*A Chloidhimh Chléirchín in Chluig* and the Concept of the Literary Cycle in Mediaeval Ireland'.

[10] The career of this unique literary patron is related by Ó hUiginn, '*Duanaire Finn*: Patron and Text'; idem, 'Somhairle Mac Domhnaill agus *Duanaire Finn*'; Walsh, 'Captain Somhairle MacDonnell and His Books'; Ó hUiginn, 'Captain Somhairle and His Books Revisited'. For additional bibliography on the patron and his books, see Ó hUiginn, '*Fiannaigheacht*, Family, Faith and Fatherland', 161 n. 69.

[11] See Ó Muraíle (ed.), *Mícheál Ó Cléirigh, His Associates and St Anthony's College, Louvain*.

al collection for Captain Mac Domhnaill that the college obtained in payment for debts or upon his death, remains in doubt. The scribe of the *duanaire*'s portion, Aodh Ó Dochartaigh, signs several colophons in the manuscript.[12] A soldier of that name, likely the same man, appears in papers relating to the regiment in which Captain Mac Domhnaill served. The colophons suggest that Ó Dochartaigh transcribed as much as he could, and ran out of material more than once, before receiving more. It is unknown how the material was obtained as Ó Dochartaigh's sources do not survive.

DF has already been mentioned as containing a copy of *AcS* and a fragment of an unnamed Fenian tale in another section bound in with the sixty-nine lays that are the focus of the present discussion. The collection travelled from Louvain to Rome during the French Revolution, and remained in Saint Isidore's College, Rome, until the collapse of the Papal States in 1870. It was smuggled from the Vatican, whence it had been taken for safety during the siege of Rome, in the British diplomatic bag, and sent to Merchants' Quay Franciscan House, Dublin.[13] Because the collection had not been in Ireland until after 1870, it was never used as a source for other manuscripts, and indeed the gulf in taste between it and later Irish tradition is significant.[14]

There is a strong antiquarian element in DF. Although a few popular lays that probably do not antedate the manuscript by more than a few decades are present towards the end, most of the collection contains earlier linguistic features (even if frequently concealed by modernisation of spelling). Murphy's commentary assigns fourteen of the poems to the late Middle Irish period of c. 1100–1200, and twenty-four more to the transitional period of 1200–1300. Recent investigation by John Carey has confirmed the general accuracy of Murphy's dates, with a suggestion that some poems may actually be earlier than Murphy thought.[15] Since DF

---

[12] Another scribe, Niall Gruamdha Ó Catháin, wrote most of the copy of *AcS* in the other part of the manuscript (A20a).

[13] The manuscript is now on deposit in UCD Archives, where it retains the shelfmark A20 that it was given at the Franciscan House of Studies, Killiney, Co. Dublin, which housed the scholarly collections assembled at Merchants' Quay, Dublin. In addition to the background information in MacNeill's introduction to *DF* i and Murphy's commentary in *DF* iii, see Dillon et al., *Catalogue of Irish Manuscripts in the Franciscan Library, Killiney*, pp. ix–xxvi and 39–45. DF proper is the second section of the manuscript, A20b.

[14] The relationships of a number of texts in DF with other lays, especially those in LL, is considered at length by Ó hUiginn in 'Duanaire Finn'.

[15] 'Remarks on Dating'. Attention has been drawn to the implications of

contains the largest assembly by far of heroic ballads of high literary quality, the present work can do no more than to delineate the general trends of the corpus and to single out a small number of poems for particular comment. Unfortunately, with very few exceptions, in-depth studies of individual poems are still lacking.[16] The collection favours narrative heroic verse. The lore poems that predominate in the *Agallamh* tradition form only a small part of DF, though the presence of a copy of *AcS* within the same manuscript certainly eliminated any need to copy these poems again in the collection of lays. The lore tradition is represented by XII 'The Household of Almha', and XLIII 'The Womenfolk of the Fian'; as well as short pedigrees in verse, such as lays XI 'The Kindred of Fionn', and XXXVII 'Fionn's Ancestry'. Genealogy also features as a major consideration in the introduction of several *féinnidhthe* in poems XLIV–XLVI. Other lays tell of the complaints of the aged Oisín and Caoilte, comparing their lot in Christian days — with the rigours of penitential fasting — to their heroic past: *Gorta chille Críonlocha, / úch, ní fhédoim a fhulang* 'The hunger of the church of Críonloch, / alas, I cannot endure it'.[17] Hardships of old age are at the centre of lyrics such as lays V, XXV, XXVI, XXVII, XXX, XXXI, XXXII, LI, LIII, and LV. Fionn makes two prophecies in lays XXXIV and XLIX. This body of lore-focused poems extends only to approximately one quarter of the *duanaire*, with the majority of it comprising heroic tales in narrative verse. Many are long adventures with plots related to the later medieval and Early Modern romances described in Chapter Five, but others focus on unique objects (XLVII 'Caoilte's Sword', VIII 'The Crane-Bag', XVI 'Caoilte's Dipper') or special places (XLII 'The Standing Stones of Ireland', XXXVIII 'The Naming of Dún Gáire').

Within the corpus of narrative adventures, DF features an unusually large number of compositions that narrate the turning points in the cycle, many of which are not preserved elsewhere. Such lays are usually late medieval and relatively uncommon. Although DF does not present them in an order progressing with the fictional chronology of the cycle, it comprises the largest

---

these conclusions for the broader understanding of the Fenian Cycle by Parsons, Review of Carey (ed.), *Duanaire Finn: Reassessments*, 72.

[16] The value of close readings of individual lays is demonstrated by Máirtín Ó Briain in studies such as '*Duanaire Finn* XII: Goll and the Champion's Portion' and 'Suirghe Fhinn' (the latter is not attested in *DF*).

[17] *DF* i, 82 (lay XXX).

corpus of milestones in the life of Fionn. This unique group deserves particular attention here. A brief verse *macgníomhartha* (lay XV) that Murphy dated to *c*. 1400 recounts an episode of the infant Fionn, here (as occasionally elsewhere) known as Glas Díghe, strangling a polecat (*toghán*) that attacked him, rather in the manner of Hercules and the serpent.[18] As in the prose tale, the lad defeats a troop of boys on the playing field, and as a result he is named in reference to the colour of his hair; here, however, it is high-king Conn who names him Fionn:

> Fiafraighis Conn na ccuradh
> fer lé ccuirthear crúas ceimionn
> cía in fionn beg bheirius báire
> ar ógaibh aille Éirionn
>
> Báoth-focal sin ar Bódhmann
> a Chuinn na ccomlann ccalma
> Is hé sútt fer na faoílti
> Fionn féin ua Baoisgne barrghlan

Conn of the champions asked — the man by whom hard marches are made — 'Who is the little *fionn* (fair lad) that wins the goal against the handsome youths of Ireland?'

'A light word is that', said Bodhmann, 'thou Conn of the brave encounters: yon lad is the man of joy, "Fionn" himself, clear-topped Ua Baoisgne'.[19]

Lay LXIX 'The Chess-game beneath the Yew-tree' is set within the tragic events of the elopement of Diarmaid and Gráinne. Diarmaid is in hiding in a yew tree, beneath which Fionn and Oisín are playing *fidhcheall*. When Oisín fails to spot a winning move, Diarmaid aids his play by dropping a berry onto the board. Diarmaid is called down under the protection of Goll when recognised by this act; and the House of Baoiscne descends into internecine strife, the first breakdown of the *fian*:

---

[18] Ibid., iii, 33.
[19] Ibid., i, 33–4, 134.

38

Ann sin tainic Díarmuid
cugainn is níorbh é ar leas
dob iomdha laoch againnc
do dícheannadh san treas.

Then Diarmaid came to us, and it was not for our good.
Many a warrior among us was beheaded in the fray.[20]

Another lay, 'Bran's Departure from the Fian' (LVI) unravels
Fionn's *geas* that governed his keeping of Bran. He struck Bran to
goad him into action; instead, *Iongnadh leis a bhualadh damh / do
bhoí athaidh gom feghadh / gur silseat frasa déra / tar a rosgaibh
rinnghéra* ('He wondered at being struck by me: for a while he
looked at me, and then streams of tears poured from his piercing
eyes'), and Bran plunged into a lough, never to be seen again.[21]
Oisín, standing at the burial cairn of his son Oscar, narrates the
events of the final Battle of Gabhair at heroic length (88qq.) in
poem XXXIX. Interestingly, there is a strong element of sympathy
for the House of Morna in DF: a group of poems focus on the
tragic figure of Goll as he prepares to make his last stand against
Fionn. 'The Wild Rush of the House of Morna' (lay XLVIII) presents the battle of Cnucha, the last victory of Clann Mhorna.
Poems III and IV present a Saul-and-David encounter of the two
warriors when their camps stand preparing for battle at dawn,
while IX and X describe Goll's musings the night before his final
combat with Fionn. He curses Clann Bhaoiscne and takes leave of
his wife to stand alone on the rocky crag. In lay XXXV, he recounts his victories to strengthen his resolve to face his fate, the
death that overtakes him in the incomplete lay XXII. At the conclusion of the fateful battles, Gabhair and Ollarbha, only the ancients remain. From a chronological standpoint, the end of the cycle
is the final exchange of Caoilte and Oisín, XIX 'The Lament for
the Fiana', enumerating the losses and downfall. It begins:

Anocht fíordheireadh ná ffían
ro sgarsat ré neart a níadh
terc anocht a ccoin sa ffir
dobadh urus a n-áirimh

---

[20] Ibid., ii, 408–9, §22.
[21] Ibid., 200–1, §12. For Bran, see Ó Briain, 'The Conception and Birth of
Fionn mac Cumhaill's Canine Cousin'.

This night 'tis an utter end of the Fiana: the power of their heroes has forsaken them; few to-night their hounds and their men: 'twere easy to number them.[22]

BDL dates a century earlier than DF, but whereas DF contains texts probably composed as far back as the twelfth century, BDL contains more modern ones.[23] This unique codex deserves a brief description. It was largely compiled near Fortingall in Perthshire, Scotland, in the early sixteenth century by James MacGregor, the titular Dean of Lismore (the island cathedral of the diocese of Argyll and the Isles) and his brother Duncan. Although there are sundry items in it, including a copy of *The Chronicle of Fortingall* — and even a grocery list — the bulk of the manuscript is a poetic collection for the enjoyment of the Dean and his circle; it assembles collections of Fenian lays, Classical bardic poetry, and vernacular Scots-Gaelic poems, in roughly similar quantities.[24] The writing is in Scottish secretary hand, rather than the usual Gaelic script of the period, and the spelling is a phonetic transcription, generally according to the spelling rules of Lowland Scots applied to the pronunciation of the local dialect. The great difficulty in deciphering the manuscript has meant that no complete edition of its texts has been produced, though most of them have been printed or edited with varying degrees of success.[25]

---

[22] Ibid., i, 47, 151.

[23] See Meek, '*Duanaire Finn* and Gaelic Scotland'.

[24] Ross, *Heroic Ballads*, numbers 29 poems as 'heroic'; Meek. 'The Corpus of Heroic Verse', identifies 27. It should also be noted that it is usual in Scottish scholarship to speak of the lays or heroic ballads in BDL as a corpus, and that practice is continued here, though several lays actually concern characters from the Ulster Cycle.

[25] The Fenian items are all printed in normalised Gaelic orthography with translations in Ross, *Heroic Ballads*; however, there are problems associated with the edition, which does not present the manuscript readings on which the restored text is based. Unaltered transcriptions of the heroic poems in the manuscript are printed in full in Campbell, *Leabhar na Feinne*. A new and comprehensive edition is in preparation by Donald Meek and William Gillies for the Scottish Gaelic Texts Society; an earlier version of this work on the ballads may be found in Meek's unpublished Ph.D. thesis 'The Corpus of Heroic Verse in the Book of the Dean of Lismore'. He has published the text of two of these lays, with normalised versions and translations in 'The Banners of the Fian in Gaelic Ballad Tradition' and 'The Death of Diarmaid in Scottish and Irish Tradition'. Also worthy of mention is the pioneering edition of M'Lauchlan, *The Dean of Lismore's Book*; the promising attempts by Cameron (*Reliquiae Celticae*, vol. i) and by Quiggin (*Poems from the Book of the Dean of Lismore*) were both cut

A single quatrain suffices to demonstrate the unique difficulties presented by this source:

Troyg lwm twllych ni faynith
Ag ni clerchew fa zeirse
Is danyth lucht ni billak
In nynit clannyth beisknyth.[26]

The quatrain in normal orthography would run thus:

Truagh liom Tulach na Féine
ag na cléirchibh fá dhaoirse;
is dána lucht na mbileog
i n-ionad Chloinne Baoiscne.

It grieves me that Tulach na Féine [the Hill of the Fian] is subjugated to the clerics; brazen are the men of the pages in the place of Clann Bhaoiscne.[27]

As already noted, the lays in BDL are of a much more modern character: there are a number of chases and adventures, rather than items concerning the 'central' plot of the cycle. Donald Meek observes that the collection is noteworthy for including an unusually high proportion of laments, which comprise half the heroic ballads in BDL; he attributes this focus to a feeling of loss for another 'heroic age' among Scottish Gaels in the aftermath of the downfall of the Lordship of the Isles in 1493. Approximately half the lays in BDL are found in later Scottish tradition, and half in later Irish collections. Although there is some overlapping of items attested in both traditions, the number preserved solely in BDL is relatively small: to judge from later manuscripts and materials gathered by eighteenth- and nineteenth-century collectors, the Dean's choices of texts form part of the mainstream of the evolving Early Modern tradition, even if his taste for the elegiac is particularly strong.[28]

---

short by their untimely deaths, resulting in incomplete posthumous publications. For an overview of the manuscript orthography and contents, see Meek, 'The Scots-Gaelic Scribes of Late Medieval Perthshire'.

[26] Campbell, *Leabhar na Feinne*, 50.

[27] Modernisation and translation based on Ross, *Heroic Poetry*, 116 (ll. 1456–60).

[28] Meek, 'The Gaelic Ballads of Scotland', 36–7. See also Meek, '*Duanaire Finn* and Gaelic Scotland'.

The choices and types of lays in BDL and DF occupy different parts of the broader tradition. The poems in DF, like those in LUM, tend to be long, not infrequently more than a hundred quatrains. It is quite clear that these texts were chanted or sung (as in the later tradition).[29] Yet, a manuscript-based element is quite apparent despite the probability of oral transmission. The narrative lays in the early collections tend to have several scenes, and they tell a complex tale on a broad scale with a literary character. Alongside these lengthy verse narratives, however, short laments or reflections, a strand of the cycle from the beginning, remained popular. In contrast, the heroic ballads in BDL are consistently short, as are the majority of Fenian lays found in later manuscripts. Each poem generally has a single linear plot and one major theme: a battle, an invasion, a challenge, a wooing, a hunt (often chasing an Otherworldly chieftain who has taken the form of an animal), an elegy, or a nostalgic recollection.[30] The range of Fenian ballads from the Early Modern period is very broad, and lays on the crucial events and battles of the cycle are evident, along with episodic adventures and reflections of the ancient Oisín.[31] Later poems that confine themselves more strictly to one theme and mood would seem to have been performed regularly; appropriate items could be found within the repertoire of a reciter to suit many types of occasion. Although it may be an oversimplification to reduce a complicated series of literary trends to a simple case of cause and effect, it is hardly a coincidence that these developments corresponded temporally with the decline of the Gaelic

---

[29] For a description of such chanting, see *DF* iii, pp. xcvi–xcvii and 132. A reference to the musical performance of these poems within BDL is found in '*Dál chabhlaigh ar Chaistéal Suibhne*' ('An assembling of a fleet [to go] against Castle Sween') which testifies that: *eachtra féine Fhinn a gceóil* 'the adventure of the Fian of Fionn [fills] their songs' (Meek, '"Norsemen and Noble Stewards"', 35 and 38, §22)

[30] A large number of lays with invader themes are collected, translated, and discussed in Christiansen, *The Vikings and the Viking Wars*, 97–387. There is analysis of the literary treatment of the motif of the hunt in Chadbourne, 'The Voices of Hounds'.

[31] Unlike the tradition of the romances analysed in the following chapter, the lays often treated crucial events, often with multiple ballads addressing them. For example, there are many ballads on the battle of Gabhair which have been addressed by Gunderloch, 'The *Cath Gabhra* Family of Ballads'. Another set, on the event of Garadh mac Morna's burning of the women of Fionn's house, which is also narrated in *AcS*, is analysed briefly by Gwynn, 'The Burning of Finn's House', 13–14, in the introduction to his edition of one of these ballads.

lordships and their courts — with the concomitant decline of the bardic orders dependent on their patronage. Nevertheless, in general there was a growth in the Gaelic literature focused on popular audiences, alongside a move from classically trained poetic writings to less professional ones, with both written and oral circulation. A metrical shift occurred at about the same time as the change in the predominant narrative style. Many late lays were composed in a metre that Torna, the first to analyse it in a scholarly fashion, called *laoidh fianaigheachta*; it has also been called the Ossianic stanza. Torna described it as being a form of quatrain in which each line has three or four stresses. The second and fourth lines rhyme, and there is *aicill* — rhyme between the final word of one line with a word in the beginning or interior of the next — within each couplet of the quatrain. To this basic form, the ornament of alliteration is frequently added. This new standard is not incompatible with the earlier syllabic metres of the *rannaigheacht* type, which also require a rhyme of the second and fourth lines (and are ornamented by alliteration, internal rhyme, and *aicill*). The difference is that the number of syllables could be irregular. The variations could be trivial as certain linguistic developments made the syllable count of older poems irregular in performance. Further variation could arise from the replacement of archaic words or phrases by alternatives. Contemporary norms of ordinary pronunciation asserted themselves in recitation. Poems were sometimes composed in, or adjusted to, variant norms of six or eight syllables. New ballads were constructed according to shifting standards. As this occurred, the number of stresses, which defined song metres, came to be taken into account as a primary metrical feature of the lays, rather than the syllable count. *Laoidh fianaigheachta* is thus a step along the path away from syllabic verse towards the stressed *amhrán* metres favoured in Modern Irish. Torna identified a number of poems in this transitional metre, including '*Agallamh Oisín agus Phádraig*' ('The Dialogue between Oisín and Patrick'), that so often opens Fenian *duanaireadha* ('poem-books'), and many of the Fenian ballads most frequently attested in eighteenth- and nineteenth-century manuscripts, such as '*Laoidh na Seilge*' ('The Lay of the Chase'), '*Cnoc an Áir*' ('The Hill of the Slaughter'), and '*Lon Doire an Chairn*' (The Blackbird of Doire an Chairn').[32] Some of the more recent lays cannot easily be read as syllabic verse at all, as the opening quatrain of '*Seilg Shléibhe gCuilinn*' ('The Chase of

---

[32] See Torna, *Filidheacht Fiannaigheachta*, 163–6.

Sliabh gCuilinn [Slieve Gullion]') demonstrates:

> Lá dá raibh Fionn, flaith,
> ar an bhfaithche i nAlmhain úir,
> do chonnairc chuige san ród
> eilit óg ar léim lúith.[33]

> One day Fionn, sovereign, / was on the green in noble Allen; / he saw coming towards him on the road / a young doe leaping nimbly.

If one were to read this quatrain as *rannaigheacht*, one would find that the first line is short by two syllables and the fourth line by one. No amount of tweaking would make the Classical requirement for the syllable-count work in this quatrain, or in many others of the poem, unless the editor were to rewrite it. Its author clearly understood it as a series of stresses:

> **Lá** dá **raibh Fionn**, **flaith**,
> ar an **bhfaith**che i n**Al**mhain **úir**,
> do **chonn**airc **chui**ge san **ród**
> **eil**it **óg** ar **léim lúith**.

Although this type of verse is a departure from the syllabic metres, *laoidh* is not merely a decayed form or an 'easy' option: in the stanza discussed here, there are four rhymes and five alliterative pairs in addition to a stress pattern.

In contrast to Modern Irish, Scots Gaelic is phonologically conservative; consequently, non-Classical syllabic verse is often better preserved in the Scottish tradition. This type of *laoidh fianaigheachta*, transitional in Irish, is the classic template for a large quantity of vernacular Scots-Gaelic poetry. This is likely a factor in the greater oral survival of lays in Scotland than in Ireland, where the manuscript tradition dominated to a much larger extent. In Scotland, there is a disconnect in the manuscript tradition after BDL, and a large number of the lays appear to have circulated orally until they were collected and printed by antiquarians in the later eighteenth and nineteenth centuries.

One ballad, recovered through transcription from oral recitation, survives from the Isle of Man, and is the sole Manx contrib-

---

[33] An Seabhac, *Laoithe na Féinne*, 74.

ution to literary *fianaigheacht*.[34] It is a fragmentary version of the burning of the Fenian women by Garadh mac Morna (here referred to as 'Orry'), a subject well represented in the Scottish repertoire.[35] The survival of the ballad hints at the continuous currency of the genre in the popular traditions of all parts of the transnational *Gaedhealtacht*. Helping the change along was the way the texts remained part of a vibrant culture, allowing for dialectal adjustment and changes to ensure comprehensibility, rather than being treated as completely fixed texts. *Mouvance*, that is to say textual evolution, must be evaluated as such, not regarded as synonymous with degeneration.[36]

The earliest version of '*Agallamh Oisín agus Phádraig*' is preserved in Duanaire Finn (lay LVII). Gerard Murphy, in his notes on the copy in that manuscript, dated it to the sixteenth century, and stated that one could emend to Classical forms, but that the syllable count would suffer; or, one could have the syllable-count and suffer many a modernism. In short, Murphy's description of the poem as *rannaigheacht* with any number of late features that defied his attempts at 'restoration' approaches the same point as Torna's understanding of the metre of the subsequent versions as *laoidh*.[37] In later tradition, this poem came to assume a central importance: it was the usual opening to collections of Fenian lays in eighteenth- and nineteenth-century manuscripts. The poem begins with Saint Patrick summoning the elderly Oisín to prayer. He is less than receptive, and starts a dialogue with Saint Patrick, consisting of various reminiscences, and stichomythia alternating understanding and disagreement (often humorous) between the two about the Fenian life and the need for

---

[34] Broderick, 'Fin as Oshin'. Three independent transcriptions of the poem are known: Douglas, Manx Museum MS 1487(d)C; BLL Additional MS (Thorkelin Collection) 11,215; the third is now lost, and known only through a facsimile. Ó Muircheartaigh, '*Fin as Ossian* Revisited', has recently drawn attention to another copy of the ballad preserved among the papers of Charles O'Conor of Belanagare.

[35] A number of related Scottish ballads are printed in Campbell, *Leabhar na Feinne*, 175–9.

[36] For discussion of textual evolution with particular regard to BDL, see Meek, 'Development and Degeneration in Gaelic Ballad Texts'. An earlier example of such differences in literary manuscripts, viz. DF and LUM, is evaluated in regard to the lay on Oscar's Sword in Flahive, '*A Chloidhimh Chléirchín in Chluig* and the Concept of the Literary Cycle in Mediaeval Ireland'.

[37] *DF* iii, 126.

repentance and prayer.[38] This lay opens a poetic anthology containing a core of sub-poems or episodes that had been assembled with care for thematic progression in which the in-tales contribute to the flow of the frame debate; this longer work, that shares the title of the opening poem, is not a mere hotch-potch with bridging quatrains, but rather 'a consistent and skilfully woven text'.[39] It circulated as a unit and 'was copied widely with little variation'.[40]

The poems, tales, and copies of the various versions of the *Agallamh* are found scattered throughout manuscripts, though only rarely accounting for more than a few items in any one codex. The Early Modern period saw the rise of *duanaireadha* associated with single scribes or patrons. DF is the earliest surviving example of one with wholly Fenian content, but by the eighteenth century, many such manuscripts were in circulation. By this time, other factors began to influence the composition of Fenian *duanaireadha*, and a common form developed to which many of them adhered closely.

It has been argued above that the exigencies of performance in an orally dominated context may have contributed to a shift towards shorter texts with simple, memorable plots. Long and elaborate heroic poems may have been less suited to the world of *seanchaidhthe* than to that of trained, literate poets providing professional entertainment for a Gaelic nobility. This is not to assert that later lays became uni-dimensional; modern scholarship has freed oral composition from claims that it either mimics the written tradition or strings along material from a common reservoir of motifs in a nearly automatic manner. Simplicity can focus emotional force; the avoidance of a multi-focal viewpoint is a deliberate aesthetic choice in folk poetry, as in written literature. As John Miles Foley observes:

> Properly managed by the poet and properly received by his or her audience, whether in the actual setting of oral traditional performance or in the still-resonant medium of the oral-derived

---

[38] See Ó Fiannachta, 'The Debate between Pádraig and Oisín'. Krause, in contrast, considers the farcical debates of the late lays as a traditional strand of long standing in 'The Hidden Oisín'. It is this element of *fianaigheacht* that led to Sir Walter Scott's literary parody in Chapter Thirty of his novel *The Antiquary*.

[39] Ní Mhurchú, '*Agallamh Oisín agus Phádraig*: Composition and Transmission', 201.

[40] Ní Mhurchú, '*Agallamh Oisín agus Phádraig*: The Growth of an Ossianic Lay', 175.

traditional text, these simple forms will bring forth enormous complexity by making present immanent associations that can never be captured in the textual net alone.[41]

The emergence of shorter, less complicated ballads must not be viewed in reductionist terms, but as part of an ongoing interaction between two strands, elite and popular, within the Gaelic tradition. The extension of the Oisín and Saint Patrick dialogue framework also provided a literary context for composition and preservation of shorter, mono-thematic texts: an episodic presentation works best when the constituent items are subordinated to the development of a larger enterprise, which was now provided. Longer and more complicated lays were less suited to such a recontextualisation. The result of how these changes finally interlocked was summarised by Pádraig Ó Fiannachta: 'The "Agallamh" [poem] offered a framework for a unified presentation of the whole corpus of Ossianic lays'.[42] The dialogue is modified and extended in some later manuscripts (with rather less concern for literary unity); and other stanzas modelled on it are used to weave together a series of many more single-plot lays into continuous texts, beyond the mark of a thousand quatrains. A few lines of banter between the ancient and the saint could effect a transition from one lay to another without a gap between them. In the later Irish manuscripts through to the time of the Famine, the presentation of Fenian poetry was more often in the unity of an extended episodic dialogue rather than a series of texts. Even when this is not so, '*Agallamh Oisín agus Phádraig*' often opens a *duanaire*, followed by a selection of other lays. An additional driving force behind this process may have been an awareness of James Macpherson's English-language Fenian-derived romance *Fingal* (discussed in Chapter Seven), but it is still fitting that the different elements of the tradition coalesced in a way that reflected closely the maturity of the literature in *AcS* six hundred years earlier.

Thousands of manuscripts with lays, frequently dominated by the work or framework of '*Agallamh Oisín agus Phádraig*', were produced between 1750 and 1850 throughout Ireland.[43] In particular, the professional Munster scribes, especially the prolific

---

[41] *Immanent Art*, 245.

[42] Ó Fiannachta, 'The Debate', 202.

[43] See Ní Mhurchú, '*Agallamh Oisín agus Phádraig*: Composition and Transmission'; examples of other collections on the same model are discussed at pp. 204–5. Ní Mhurchú is working on a semi-diplomatic edition of this collection of lays as preserved in RIA Stowe MS A iv 2 (27).

Ó Longáin family, turned out a vast number of manuscript copies. Many hundreds remain in Ireland, in Britain, and in the countries where Irish emigrants went; many manuscript libraries can boast of several such compilations, and a significant number remain in private hands.[44] The presentation of the later poetry in this format has carried through from the manuscripts into many popular printed collections. Since these ballads are, of the entire Fenian Cycle, the most linguistically accessible literature to a present-day reader of Irish, and also because they are widely translated in anthologies, it would be superfluous to produce exhaustive lists and summaries here.[45] Nevertheless, the state of the field is not what one may assume from this fact. A handful of favourite poems are printed and reprinted, but the corpus easily extends to thousands of lays, though no reliable estimate of its extent has been produced: there is no index or guide to the poems that languish unedited. To set the study of the late medieval and Early Modern tradition of Fenian lays on a solid scholarly basis would require many years of teamwork backed by a major academic institution. Despite the occasional interest shown by scholars in individual lays, no major projects to investigate this corpus, systematically identifying and editing the ballads, are in progress. To conclude this section, it is appropriate to state the obvious: from the time of *AcS* to the collapse of the native literary tradition, the Fenian Cycle generally has a predominance of verse; and the narrative lay or heroic ballad, attested in manuscripts as far back as LL, has been the most productive form for *fianaigheacht* from the close of the Middle Irish period until new composition ceased with the decline of literary Irish in the eighteenth century.[46]

---

[44] A typical example is described in Gillies, 'An Irish Manuscript in Scotland'.

[45] O'Daly, 'Laoithe Fiannuigheachta' and 'Laoithe Fiannuigheachta ... Second Series' were the first major Irish attempts to print the lays; the first series is an extended '*Agallamh Oisín agus Phádraig*', while the second is a compendium. Later popular collections, although they often insert titles between the items, link the texts as progressions or as though they are chapters of one whole. Examples of these include: O'Kelly, *Leabhar na Laoitheadh*; Torna, *Filidheacht Fiannaigheachta*; a modernised school edition of Torna's work, *Filíocht Fianaíochta*; Ó Donnchadha (Torna), *Óirchiste Fiannuíochta*. More lays of this type are edited separately in Laoide, *Fian-laoithe* and in An Seabhac, *Laoithe na Féinne*. Noteworthy editions of the individual poems in the tradition of '*Agallamh Oisín agus Phádraig*' from Irish sources only are listed in Ní Mhurchú, '*Agallamh Oisín agus Phádraig*: Composition and Transmission', 206–8.

[46] See Breatnach, 'The End of a Tradition'.

5. Early Modern Romances

The main direction of development of Fenian-Cycle prose works after *AcS* was altogether different from that of the lays. Early Modern Irish tales were highly influenced in style and form by European models of romance employed widely in French and English. Irish adaptation of these conventions nativised them, incorporating certain features of earlier Irish narrative technique, such as ornamental verse. Later Fenian tales cleave more closely to the form of the romance, which was a template in general use for tales in all the cycles; the conventions of presentation that had evolved for Fenian poetry continued to develop separately.[1]

One of the oldest prose Fenian tales after *AcS* is 'The Chase of Síodh na mBan Fionn and the Death of Fionn' in BLL Egerton MS 1782. This bears a colophon dated 1419; its text may be slightly earlier than the surviving copy.[2] This narrative points the direction that the prose of the cycle would take in subsequent centuries. Opening with a series of lore recitations by Fionn, and incorporating a plot whose structure is dictated by the geography of the chase, the narration is similar in style to the *Agallamh* tradition. However, this tale dispenses altogether with the Patrician frame and speaks with the external third-person narrator usual to most medieval Irish tales and to later prose romances. It favours an expanded retelling of events known in the earlier tradition, and is narrated as a tale rather than as the reminiscence of an aged survivor (the latter is usual in the lays).

Prose romances have a fairly set form and content. In many, their style is ornamented with long alliterative descriptive passages or groupings of synonyms. Over time these characteristics became more pronounced, to the extent that in the seventeenth century, when the form had evolved fully, it began to approach self-caricature. The prose grew increasingly elaborate, and many

---

[1] For additional discussion of the Fenian romances in the context of the wider romantic literature, see Bruford, *Gaelic Folk-tales and Mediaeval Romances*; and also Murphy, *The Ossianic Lore and Romantic Tales*, esp. 49–55. Useful criticism of some assumptions made by these scholars has been provided in the study of a non-Fenian romance, *Serc Duibhe Lacha do Mhongán* ('The Love of Dubh Lacha for Mongán'), by Nagy, 'In Defence of Rómánsaíocht'.

[2] Ed. and trans. by Meyer, *Fianaigecht*, 52–99. Meyer placed it in a list of items that he considered to be of the thirteenth and fourteenth centuries but did not attempt to date it more precisely. The language is Early Modern Irish with a few petrified commonplaces from Middle Irish.

earlier romances, originally less florid, exhibit stylistic alteration in later copies. Such reworkings mean that copies of the same story, though they frequently match sentence for sentence, seldom match word for word.[3] The incorporation of poetry within the romances, whether recited by a character or used to highlight important turns of plot, is a feature of most such texts, though a substantial minority lack the embellishment of verse.[4] The plots of nearly all are episodic in nature. Many have storylines focused on a foreign invader or Otherworldly foe; a number of others involve a series of loosely related adventures encountered on a journey or quest. Pursuits and chases can either provide the main plot or bind together a series of encounters to extend a tale. A mere handful of devices can be used to create a potentially infinite number of episodes that may be related in any order with no noticeable loss of cohesion. Though Fionn may lose thousands of men in battles, overcoming innumerable threats, none of his core group of warriors is slain in the adventures: the set cast of characters must live to fight again. Romances almost never tell of crucial developments in the broader cycle nor treat 'the residuum proper to Fionn'; rather, they narrate episodes within a vague heyday of the *fian*. In this regard, the best-known text in the genre, *Tóraigheacht Dhiarmada agus Ghráinne* ('The Pursuit of Diarmaid and Gráinne') — a reworking of an older story — is unique for incorporating the death of Diarmaid, a character of some importance in other texts within the cycle. Had it not been part of an inherited plot, it is unlikely that any romance writer would have conceived of introducing any such development. In short, the plots of many romances have much in common thematically with international folktales, and the developments frequently appear to have borrowed from what is characteristically folkloric tradition, resulting in the literary and oral strands of the tradition being 'inextricably interwoven' in such texts.[5]

One of the most popular Fenian romances, *Bruidhean Bheag na hAlmhaine* ('The Little Brawl of Almha'), demonstrates well the serial nature of romance storylines.[6] In this case, the action

---

[3] For more discussion, including a rather extreme example of scribal expansion, see Breatnach, 'Early Modern Irish Prose', 204–5, §5.6.

[4] A notable example of a romance in prose alone is *Eachtra Lomnochtáin*, which fills 96 pages in the edition of Bergin and MacNeill.

[5] Bruford, 'Oral and Literary Fenian Tales', 56; see in particular the motif list at p. 31.

[6] The text is preserved in more than forty manuscripts. The earliest is NLS Adv. MS 72.1.34 (Gaelic MS XXXIV; *olim* Kilbride MS 3), generally

springs from the well-known hostility between Clann Bhaoiscne and Clann Mhorna. Fionn gets into an argument during a feast at his stronghold, Almha, when Goll rewards the poet Fearghus with tribute that he got from Lochlann. The argument as to whether it is right that Goll should receive tributes independently opens old wounds: the story of how the tribute was imposed relates to the events leading to the overthrow and killing of Fionn's father, Cumhall. In the mêlée that breaks out in the hall, 1,100 of Fionn's people are slain (though not a single one of them has a recognisable name); Clann Mhorna lose only 56. Fearghus intervenes to stop the fight, and the conflict is referred to the royal judges Flaithrí and Fíthiol for a full, just resolution. They hold that Goll was in the right, but that Fionn, having been suitably punished by the result of the brawl, is not liable for any additional damages. Peace is patched together, and the *fiana* go on as if nothing had happened: in the end, one has a tale rooted in the ongoing rivalry of Clann Bhaoiscne and Clann Mhorna, but no final move towards a full breach between Fionn and Goll. The text falls into distinct scenes. The first describes the grandeur of Fionn's hall in great detail: gold, silver, the seating arrangements, the rich attire of the guests, and the splendour of the feast:

Is ann sin do éirigh feadhmanntuigh go fíoréasgaidhe re freastal ⁊ frighóladh na sluagh ⁊ na sochaidhe, ⁊ cuirn chlochabhuadhach[a] chaomhadha leó go ngeimamhlaibh gnaoiamhla gloinidhe ⁊ go ceartacht chaomh chruth-niamhdha for gach leastar loinnearrdha lán-áluinn dhóibh, ⁊ do dháiliotar deocha diana díomsacha dona deagh-laochaibh ⁊ biadha núath neamhearrsaidhe dona féinneadhaibh go foistinach fíor-aibéil.[7]

Then the servants stood swiftly indeed to attend and minister to the hosts and multitude, and they had precious, stone-encrusted

---

known as the Dunstaffnage Manuscript, dated 1603. A list of the manuscript copies of Early Modern romances is given in Bruford, *Gaelic Folk-tales and Mediaeval Romances*, 250–67, as well as a summary table at pp. 70–1. All estimations of numbers of manuscript copies of tales in the notes below are based on Bruford, though slightly modified due to inclusion of materials catalogued since. Three versions have been published: O'Grady from BLL Additional MS 18,747 in *Silva Gadelica*, ed. i, 336–42, trans. ii, 378–85; ed. Ní Shéaghdha from the Dunstaffnage Manuscript, 'Bruighion Bheag na hAlmhan'; ed. Ó Gallchobhair, from Maynooth, Russell Library, MS 3.e.18 (with variants from other Maynooth copies), 'Bruighean Bheag na h-Almhaine' (this last version is normalised).

[7] Ní Shéaghdha, 'Bruighion Bheag na hAlmhan', 18.

drinking-horns with clear delightful gems and with glisten-
ingly-wrought goldsmithing on each brilliant, truly splendid
vessel of them, and they served very potent potables to the
good warriors and favourable fresh foods to the Fenians grace-
fully and promptly.[8]

The second part is Goll's story of how he received the tribute. The
ensuing conflict dominates the third. It is divided into a series of
sketches, naming and describing a warrior, then his weapons, and
then the mighty blows he strikes that night. Fighting tends to be
described as single combat, even in the thick of battle; realistic
descriptions of fighting technique are not a feature of the genre,
and such stretches of the battle scene (as are not merely strings of
adjectives describing a warrior) possess this tenor:

Is ann sin do chomhraic Oscur ₇ Conán re chéile; ₇ do bodh
neartmhar neamhthláith nemhneach naimhdeamhuil niadh-
mhiscneach an comhlann lán sin, ₇ do bhean Oscar osnadh
eugcomhlainn as Chonán fá gheóigh; ₇ do fheuch Conán ar Art
óg mac Morna; ₇ nír fuiluingeadh sin le hArt óg, uair do éirigh
go healamh úrmhaisneach, ₇ do-chuaidh ina éideadh gan fhuirach, ₇ do gonadh Os[car] go nimhneach neartchalma ré hArt; ₇
níor fulaingeadh sin le hOisín fearamhuil fíorárrachtach mac
Finn, uair do ghabh airm ₇ éideadh chatha chuige, ₇ do-chuaidh
isin n-iorghail gan fhuirach, ₇ tug guin ghuasachtach dho-
fhulaing ar Art óg mac Morna.[9]

Then Oscar and Conán fought each other; and that full combat
was mighty, unamiable, deadly, hostile, heroically rancorous;
and Oscar obtained a groan of anguish from Conán in the end;
and Conán looked at young Art mac Morna; that was not
endured by young Art, whereby he arose promptly and resol-
utely, and he put on his armour without delay, and Oscar was
wounded sorely with wonderous force by Art; this was not
endured by virile, truly doughty Oisín, son of Fionn, whereby
he donned arms and battle-armour, and he went into the fray
without delay, and he gave a perilous insufferable wound to
young Art mac Morna.

---

[8] Translations here and elsewhere in this chapter when no source is specified
are by the author.
[9] Ibid., 29.

The last scene is the resolution with a legal judgment, which, after some lengthy discussion, restores the *status quo ante*. Most of the romances contain a rather small number of fixed plot forms. For the purposes of this discussion, three primary types may be identified, with notable variants following; a few representative texts have been chosen as examples to illustrate each type. In the ensuing remarks, it is certainly not possible to list, never mind discuss, all the romances in each category.

The first plot type is the pursuit (*tóraigheacht*), which involves the Fenians chasing a character and which usually leads to secondary adventures on the way. *Tóraigheacht Dhiarmada agus Ghráinne* is the only romance that is also the death tale of a Fenian warrior.[10] It relates the elopement of Gráinne, daughter of high-king Cormac, with Diarmaid — on the night of her wedding to Fionn. The pair flee across Ireland with a vengeful Fionn in pursuit, until peace is restored by the Otherworldly king Aonghus. Fionn, however, is not contented, and years later convinces Diarmaid to hunt a boar with him. Diarmaid does so, though it is a *geas* (taboo) for him; the consequences prove fatal. The tale is an Early Modern version of a much older story, of which the name is preserved in the tale-lists, *Aithed Granne ingine Corbmaic la Diarmaid ua Duibhne* ('The Elopement of Gráinne, Daughter of Cormac, with Diarmaid ua Duibhne').[11] An episode from this earlier version is preserved as the short tale *Uath Beinne Étair* ('The Terror of Howth'),[12] in addition to other fragments and references. The poet Gearóid Iarla (†1398) refers to Diarmaid and

---

[10] The earliest witness is Dublin RIA MS 24 P 9 (739), dated 1651; late manuscripts are numerous. Among the editions of the text, three are worthy of note here: Ní Shéaghdha's Irish Texts Society volume *Tóruigheacht Dhiarmada agus Ghráinne* is a semi-diplomatic edition of 24 P 9; Ní Shéaghdha, *Tóraigheacht Dhiarmada agus Gráinne* is a normalised text based on a number of manuscripts with glossary and notes for the general reader. A very different version is presented in O'Grady, '*Toruigheacht Dhiarmada agus Ghrainne*'. Breatnach has examined the textual transmission and many manuscript variants of this romance in 'The Transmission and Text of *Tóruigheacht Dhiarmada agus Ghráinne*: A Reappraisal', drawing particular attention to the longer version in RIA MS 23 L 39 (114) (dated 1737–8), which is similar to O'Grady's edition from a lost manuscript. He considers that this version may preserve original material not found in 24 P 9, the earliest witness. Additional literary discussion is to be found in Ó Cathasaigh, 'Tóraíocht Dhiarmada agus Ghráinne'.

[11] Mac Cana, *The Learned Tales*, 57.

[12] Published in Ní Shéaghdha, *Tóruigheacht Dhiarmada agus Ghráinne*, 130–7.

Gráinne frequently; his references match the romance rather than the fragments of the older tale, though this could be due to intermediate versions. A number of lays also explore aspects of the flight of Diarmaid and Gráinne, often taking the form of addresses or dialogues.[13] Of the romances, *Tóraigheacht Dhiarmada agus Ghráinne* is certainly the best known, perhaps because its intrinsic plot seems more satisfying than many others to the modern reader.[14]

Tóraigheacht Shaidhbhe Inghine Eoghain Óig ('The Pursuit of Sadhbh, Daughter of Young Eoghan')[15] is a chase of a different nature altogether: the Fenians undertake the pursuit of Sadhbh, wife of the *féinnidh* Glas, to rescue her from Ciotach, king of Dreollann, who has abducted her. The Fenians pursue her through various adventures to Dreollann and return with her, but they do not encounter Ciotach, who is away. He returns in a second episode, in which he attempts revenge by invading Ireland. Like many an invader, he is dispatched by Oscar, though not without a good battle first.

A variant of the *tóraigheacht*-type must be noted in *Eachtra Lomnochtáin an tSléibhe Riffe* ('The Adventure of Lomnochtán of Sliabh Riffe')[16] and *Tóraigheacht* [or *Eachtra*] *an Ghiolla Dheacair* ('Pursuit [or Adventure] of the Troublesome Lad').[17] In these tales, the eponymous characters entice the Fenians abroad into a

---

[13] Some examples of this poetry: Murphy, *Early Irish Lyrics*, §§54–5 (§55 is a restored version of *DF* lay XXXIII); a complaint from Diarmaid to Gráinne in BDL is printed in Ross, *Heroic Poetry*, 176 9 (ll. 2253–92); three Irish lays of Diarmaid are printed in An Seabhac, *Laoithe na Féinne*, 274–7; and many items from Scottish collections are printed in Campbell, *Leabhar na Feinne*, 151–64.

[14] This popularity is also due in part to the fact that, in the past, both the *Tóraigheacht* and *Bruidhean Chaorthainn* were prescribed texts for the Leaving Certificate examination.

[15] The text is found in more than fifty manuscripts; it has been edited by Ua Cuain.

[16] Ed. Bergin and MacNeill. The protagonist's name has been unofficially translated as 'Starkers'.

[17] There are at least forty manuscript copies extant. Four different texts, each from a single witness, have been published: O'Grady, *Silva Gadelica*, ed. i, 257–75, trans. ii, 292–311, from BLL Additional MS 34,119; ed. Ua hÓgáin and Laoide, from a Waterford manuscript, in *Teacht ⁊ Imtheacht an Ghiolla Dheacair*; ed. An Seabhac, *Tóraidheacht an Ghiolla Dheacair*, from RIA MS 24 B 28 (244) (misprinted as 24 B 38 in the introduction); ed. Ó Canainn, in *Diarmuid ⁊ Gráinne / An Giolla Deacair / Bodach an Chóta Lachtna*, 66–108, from NLI MS G. 230, which is very closely related to An Seabhac's text. There is also an abridged translation in Joyce, *Old Celtic Romances*, 154–85.

set of adventures (for there are always digressions on the way...).
Kingdoms such as Sorcha and Tír fo Thuinn ('Land Beneath the
Wave') in *Tóraigheacht an Ghiolla Dheacair* are described in
magical terms; these appear to be the successors to the enchanted
lands of *Immram Brain*, *Immram Curaig Maíle Dúin*, and *Immram
Curaig Ua Corra* ('The Voyage of Bran', 'The Voyage of Mael
Dúin's Curragh', and 'The Voyage of Uí Chorra's Curragh').
Additionally, it should be noted that the Giolla Deacair identifies
himself as being of the Fomhoire, the Otherworldly race
traditionally opposed to the Tuatha Dé Danann. These tales form a
thematic bridge to the next type, the *bruidhean*.

The *bruidhean* typifies a second common type of plot in
late medieval and Early Modern tales. Although the root meaning
of the word is 'hostel, (banqueting) hall, or (Otherworld) palace',
it came to have a secondary sense of 'a brawl [usually at a feast in
such a building]'. In romances, the meaning has been honed more
precisely still: these are tales that centre around a trap, almost
always Otherworldly in nature. The Fenians either happen upon,
or are more frequently enticed into, a fortress, where their expected entertainment takes on a sinister aspect when the hostility of
their host becomes manifest. The unfolding of the plot thereafter
hinges upon how the Fenians free themselves or are freed, bringing about the expected mêlée within the hall.[18]

Bruidhean Chaorthainn ('The Rowan-Tree Hostel') tells the
story of Míogach, son of a king of Lochlann who is defeated by
Fionn, pitied by him and invited to settle in Ireland.[19] Years later,
he wreaks his revenge by glueing the Fenians in place when they
attend a feast he gives. Hearing the *dord fiansa* (the summoning
call), Oisín, who had been absent, sends men to aid them. Of
course, the enchantment is not easily broken, requiring the blood
of three princes, which Diarmaid duly acquires in a series of
adventures. Naturally, a final battle between the *fiana* and their

---

[18] Ó Cróinín, 'Bruíonta na Féinne', contains a discussion of the plot type with
especial reference to the tales *Bruidhean Chéise Corainn*, *Bruidhean
Chaorthainn*, *Bruidhean Eochaidh Bhig Dheirg*, and *Bruidhean Bheag na
hAlmhaine*. The earliest extant example of this tale-type is 'Find and the
Phantoms' (discussed above pp. 18–20).

[19] The only edition of this text is Mac Piarais, *Bruidhean Chaorthainn*. It was
prepared from two eighteenth-century manuscripts in the RIA. Excerpts of a
seventeenth-century copy in the Dunstaffnage MS have been published in
Campbell, *Leabhar na Feinne*, 86–8; this version contains verse not found
in Mac Piarais' text, and it still awaits a full edition. There are nearly eighty
known copies in manuscript. A loose translation from an unidentified
manuscript may be found in Joyce, *Old Celtic Romances*, 123–53.

'hosts' results. Although there is a long series of heroic single combats at the ford in front of the hostel, much of the appeal of the story lies in humour, in episodes such as feeding Conán when he is stuck by pouring drink through the roof; or Conán losing the skin of his rear when forcefully pulled free.[20] *Bruidhean Chéise Chorainn* ('The Brawl of Céis Chorainn') is a story of much the same character.[21] Here it is an angry Otherworldly chieftain who entraps the Fenians on the hunt with the help of the enchantment of his three daughters. This time, it is Goll who is not present, and who fights the magical daughters, killing two and blinding one. The blinded sister promises to free the Fenians in return for her life, but as soon as she has done so, she returns to fight Goll again! (What would a romance be without a final battle?) Naturally, she shares in the fate of her sisters. There are many other tales that make use of this plot formula. A number of these are also reflected in the lays, for example, the tale *Bruidhean Eochaidh Bhig Dheirg* ('The Brawl of Little Red Eochaidh') narrates the same events as the poem '*Laoidh an Chon Duibh*' (or '*Laoidh na Con Duibhe*') 'Lay of the Black Hound'.[22]

One of the stories best attested in the manuscript tradition is *Feis Tighe Chonáin* ('The Feast of Conán's House').[23] It is a variation of the *bruidhean*-type tale, in that the hosteller Conán (not the same Conán as in *Bruidhean Chaorthainn*), contrary to the usual pattern, is not the enemy, though he has a history of hostility towards Fionn. The Fenians, having been hunting, find themselves deep in the wilderness; at dusk, they happen upon Conán's hostel. In the evening's entertainments, Fionn is bound by *geasa* to recite a number of tales about his youth and the adventures of the *fiana*. He then claims the hand of Conán's daughter, Finndealbh, and a

---

[20] Pearse (Mac Piarais), requiring that Irish literature be morally pure, silently rewrote this episode in the only published edition. Bruford found that this bawdy scene was present in all manuscript copies that he consulted (*Gaelic Folk-tales and Mediaeval Romances*, 3–4 and 115–16).

[21] Nearly seventy copies in manuscript are known. O'Grady published the text from BLL Additional MS 18,747 in *Silva Gadelica*, ed. i, 306–10; trans. ii, 343–7, giving the romanticised English title 'The Enchanted Cave of Keshcorran' to his translation. Ó Gallchobhair presents a normalised text in 'Bruighean Chéise Corainn'.

[22] The tale is found in more than thirty manuscripts; the oldest dated copy is TCD MS H.5.28 (1399). The lay is printed in An Seabhac, *Laoithe na Féinne*, 170–5. For a comparison of the plots, see Bruford, *Gaelic Folk-tales and Mediaeval Romances*, 117–18.

[23] There are at least fifty extant manuscript copies. Ed. Joynt, *Feis Tighe Chonáin*; ed. and trans. O'Kearney, 'Feis Tighe Chonain Chinn-Shleibhe'.

thousand *féinnidhthe* gather for the wedding-feast. While the company is assembling, two members of the Tuatha Dé Danann in the retinue of the high-king take offence at the space allocated to them in the hostel, which is filled to bursting with the revelling Fenian host; in addition, they claim that Finndealbh was already espoused to one of the Tuatha Dé Danann. Insulted, they depart and summon their hostile kin to attack the hostel. In the final battle, the Tuatha Dé Danann are defeated, though the *fiana* suffer heavy losses. The interest of the romance lies chiefly in the numerous in-tales and items of lore recited by Fionn and the Fenians during their entertainment; the tale's frame is brief by comparison, and the battle — the summit of the main plot — is sketched out in a single paragraph.

Several examples of this tale type overlap with *eachtra*-type romances. *Cuireadh Mhaoil Uí Mhanannáin* ('Maol Ua Manannáin's Invitation'),[24] a late example, has been identified by Alan Bruford as a Fenian reworking of what is frequently referred to as 'Cormac's Otherworldly Adventure' (*Eachtra Chormaic* ['Cormac's Adventure']) or 'The Obtaining of Cormac's Branch' (*Fagháil Craoibhe Cormaic*).[25] For a *bruidhean*, the Otherworldly palace of this romance is rather benign, but the Fenians have been brought there to learn a lesson.

The last category of romances consists of the attempts of foreign marauders (not infrequently Otherworldly) to invade Ireland. Among these, *Eachtra Thaile mhic Thréun* ('The Adventure of Talc son of Treon'), is worthy of mention as a romance that interweaves closely with other aspects of the tradition.[26] The Fenian lay *'Cnoc an Áir'* ('The Hill of the Slaughter') summarises the events of Talc's attempted invasion of Ireland; mentions of Talc are numerous in the corpus of Early Modern lays.[27] Talc's attack also features as an episode in *'Laoidh Mheargaigh na Lann'* ('The Lay of Meargach of the Blades'), but even a glance through the

---

[24] In RIA MSS 23 I 48 (942) and 23 K 3 (68); ed. Hyde and Ó Caomhánaigh, 'Cuireadh Mhaoil Uí Mhananáin'.

[25] Bruford, *Gaelic Folk-tales and Mediaeval Romances*, 50.

[26] Attested only in one manuscript, recorded as being privately owned by Fr L. O'Donellan of Crossmaglen, Co. Armagh, at the time the edition was made (1952); it is now Belfast, Coláiste Mhaolmhaodhóg, LS Uí Thuathail 1. The manuscript dates from the nineteenth century, but copies the colophon of its exemplar, dated 1729. Ed. in Ní Mhuirgheasa and Ó Ceithearnaigh, *Sgéalta Rómánsuíochta*, 241–99.

[27] An Seabhac, *Laoithe na Féinne*, 30–1. A later version of the text is printed in O'Kelly, *Leabhar na Laoitheadh*, 28–38.

indices of any published collection of lays will yield many an additional reference to the events of this story, which was evidently well-known.[28] The best-known example in this category, however, is *Cath Fionntrágha* ('The Battle of Ventry').[29] Therein, Dáire Donn, having conquered the rest of the world, sets his sights on Ireland. The tale is thus one that is driven by the great battle in which the Fenians defeat Dáire, king of the World. The romance has an additional focus in the love of the warrior Caol for the maiden Geilghéis. Caol is a hero who is killed in action; Geilghéis nurses the wounded, but dies of a broken heart. These characters provide a tragic human interest against the background of battle. The romance is built around earlier traditions concerning the conflict at Ventry, which first figures in *AcS*.[30] A version of this tale is also preserved in a lay unique to BDL, though the details do not match between any of these versions.[31]

Romances may frequently be extended by addition of extra incidents or by being knitted together in a series. Some examples of such in-tales or diversionary adventure have already been noted and are especially frequent in the *eachtra*-type. A fine example of a substantial romance constructed by such addition is the seventeenth-century *Imtheacht an Dá Nónbhar agus Tóraigheacht Taise Taoibhghile* ('The Expedition of the Two Ninesomes and the Pursuit of Taise White-side'), which extends to the size of a modern novel.[32] Very few of the longer romances are without such digressions, and plots — seldom the driving force of such tales — are rarely linear and logical.

---

[28] An Seabhac, *Laoithe na Féinne*, 32–3. See also O'Kelly, *Leabhar na Laoitheadh*, 38–45; the Talc episode is much reduced in O'Kelly's version.

[29] Ed. and trans. Meyer, *Cath Finntrága*; ed. O'Rahilly, *Cath Finntrágha*. Both editions are based on BLO Rawlinson MS B. 487 (*c*. 1460). A later version found in more than fifty manuscripts has not been printed, although some variants from one such, BLL Egerton MS 149, are given in Meyer's appendix. A recent analysis of the text with discussion of other traditions regarding this battle is Breatnach, 'Cath Fionntrágha'.

[30] Ó Coileáin, 'The Setting of *Géisid Cúan*', has made the case that *AcS*'s prose in-tale, which is set in Kerry, has taken in a pre-existing poem '*Géisid Cúan*' ('The Haven Roars'), which was originally set elsewhere. Breatnach has placed the origins of the romance in Sligo in 'The Historical Context of *Cath Fionntrágha*', arguing that it is an allegory of the doings of the Ó Domhnaill lords of that area and Clann tSuibhne contemporary with the Rawlinson manuscript of the tale; this explains the paucity of specific Kerry topography in the earliest version of the romance.

[31] Printed in Campbell, *Leabhar na Feinne*, 137–8; normalised and translated in Ross, *Heroic Poetry*, 18–29 (ll. 169–336).

[32] Ed. Ní Mhuirgheasa.

The most comprehensive study of the Early Modern romances to date, in which lists of constituent texts (not merely Fenian ones) are given by theme, is Alan Bruford's *Gaelic Folk-tales and Mediaeval Romances*.[33] Bruford observes that the earliest texts tend to be the most literary as well as the most developed. The generally poorer plots of later romances were combined with an increasingly stodgy prose style. The reworking of traditional plots and themes, polished and written according to the conventions of this tale-type, gradually ceased in the eighteenth century. When the conventions of the romance faded from productivity, no new model for composition succeeded it, and the creation of new literary prose *fianaigheacht* dwindled away. Nevertheless, as Bruford stresses, the romances did not die altogether. The Early Modern romances had a wide manuscript circulation until the beginning of the twentieth century as well as an afterlife in oral tradition.

Bruford's observations are derived from an unrivalled personal knowledge of the large corpus of late medieval and Early Modern romances in manuscript as well as in print; a large portion of the corpus of romances remains unpublished, and only a handful of texts have seen a modern edition. In the forty years since Bruford's monograph, the number of manuscripts catalogued has increased greatly, and many a late manuscript has turned up since, still awaiting scholarly attention; yet new editions of Fenian romances have not been forthcoming since Ní Shéaghdha's 1967 *Tóruigheacht Dhiarmada agus Ghráinne*. It is unlikely that a more comprehensive evaluation of such literature will be undertaken until significant strides are made in the publication of material. The Early Modern romances are among the least-studied texts in Irish literature, and the paucity of relevant scholarship hinders understanding of this important part of the Fenian Cycle.

---

[33] The Fenian romances are described in Chapters 9–11.

6. Antiquarians and Historians

Historians of the seventeenth century accepted the medieval fiction of Fionn as a third-century military officer, and they stressed this strand of the tradition, thereby concealing the Otherworldly aspects of Fionn, his warriors, and their adventures — elements totally unacceptable to the theologically dominated worldviews of the Reformation and Counter-reformation. *The Annals of the Four Masters* (completed in 1636), following *The Annals of Tigernach* and *The Annals of Ulster*, record Fionn's death at Áth Brea on the Boyne at the hands of Aichleach mac Duibhdhreann and the Luaighne Teamhrach in 283 AD. *The Annals of the Four Masters*, however, sees fit to include additional Fenian entries: the next year, Cairbre Lifeachair is slain in Cath Gabhra; and in 285, it is stated that the Fenian warrior Caoilte mac Rónáin slew high-king Fothadh Airgtheach in the battle of Ollarbha.[1] The antiquarian Dubhaltach Mac Fhirbhisigh, one of the last generation in Ireland to possess a bardic education, collected and tidied the genealogies of the Fenians in his *magnum opus*, *Leabhar Mór na nGenealach*, among the families, clans, kings, and saints of Ireland.[2] In this period, the Clann Chaimbéil (Campbells) of Argyll created an alternative pedigree for itself in the popular tradition, claiming descent from the Fenian warrior Diarmaid ua Duibhne, although they had long possessed a different noble descent that was well documented in the learned spheres of the time.[3] All of these texts approach the *fiana* with caution: they accept historicity, but they pass over the tales and lays in silence.

One author, however, departed from this approach and took a less cautious stance. Geoffrey Keating engaged extensively with medieval *fianaigheacht*, incorporating long passages into his work and modernising the earlier tales that captured the minds of generations of readers. Consequently, scholarship wrote Fionn and his *fian* into history quite solidly — at least until the advent of the twentieth century. Despite this, Keating dismissed romances as exactly that, and tried to retrieve an 'historical' core:

---

[1] O'Donovan, *Annála Ríoghachta Éireann*, i, 118–21.

[2] Ó Muraíle, *Leabhar Mór na nGenealach*, ii, 304, §483.23; ii, 196–8, §§434.4–436.5. Ó Muraíle's indices list a number of additional passing mentions of Fionn elsewhere in the work. Amongst these, the most notable is a genealogical poem attributed to Fionn in vol. ii, 678, §§680.8–11.

[3] See Gillies, 'Heroes and Ancestors'.

is follus nach fuil agus nach raibhe meas stáire fírinnighe ag na seanchadhaibh ar chath Fionntrágha, acht gurab dearbh leo gurab finnsceul filidheachta do cumadh mar chaitheamh aimsire é.

it is clear that the 'shanachies' [antiquaries] do not, and did not, regard the Battle of Ventry as a true history, but that they are assured that it is a poetical romance, which was invented as a pastime.[4]

Keating argued strongly for an historical place for the *fiana*. He moved beyond the annalistic and genealogical statements current in the learned schools to use three categories of historical evidence: oral tradition, written histories, and *monumenta* (in which category he places the archaeological evidence of ruins and the place-names associated with them). On this basis, he found that the *fiana* had been *buannadha do ríoghaibh Éireann* ('hired warriors to the kings of Ireland').[5] He continues with an extended description of this army, its numbers and organisation, and its customs; for example he explained *fulachta fiadha* 'wilderness cooking-pits' (also popularly called *fulachta fian* 'cooking-places of the *fian*') as being associated with them. This passage closes with a lengthy description of the extraordinary qualities required of a prospective *féinnidh*, which is mostly a paraphrase of *Áirem Muintire Finn*.[6]

The political and religious upheavals of this period changed both the circumstances of the literature and the ways in which it was understood. As the concluding paragraphs of Chapters Four and Five relate in regard to the poetry and the prose romances, the learned Gaelic elite of Ireland slowly faded away in the seventeenth century, and the eighteenth century saw the eclipse of many forms of literary composition. In Scotland, the literate Gaelic population was substantially smaller but held out longer; the last vestiges of the old order continued until the aftermath of the rebellion of 1745. Thereafter, the decline of traditional Fenian composition was underway, even though it took two centuries to reduce it from a torrent to a trickle; on the other hand, the oral tradition withstood these pressures with greater success, ensuring that the audience for this material did not fully disappear and aiding in its preservation.

---

[4] Céitinn, *Foras Feasa ar Éirinn*, i, 50–1.
[5] Ibid., ii, 326–7.
[6] Ibid., ii, 326–35; cf. pp. 16–17 above.

Fenian literature remained important among the people, and became enshrined in the self-identification of the Gaelic nations in the seventeenth century. Indeed, Mícheál Mac Craith has demonstrated that the re-enforced nationalist symbolism of Fionn as hero of Ireland was put to use almost immediately as a literary model for Tadhg Ó Cianáin's account of the Flight of the Earls, in which the Ó Domhnaill's flight to Rome (1607) is portrayed as an heroic adventure.[7] In his most recent exploration of the scholarly reasons that may have underlain the writing of DF (including the copy of *AcS* bound with it), as well as noting the self-identification of its patron (Captain Somhairle Mac Domhnaill) as a kind of latter-day *féinnidh*, Ruairí Ó hUiginn concludes that 'it may have been compiled, not out of any sentimental or antiquarian interest, but in the spirit of an emerging nationalism'.[8]

The shared approaches of the traditional genealogists, representing the views passed through the late medieval and Early Modern learned schools, and of Keating, who took a less critical approach to his sources based on the test of plausibility, represent the default position current among Irish and Scots-Gaelic speakers. There was no dissent from the view that Fenians were historical personages upon whom there was legendary accretion. The sole difference lay in the estimate of the extent of fantastic accretion. Although the quantity of learned and literary material from the Gaelic languages that crossed the gap into scholarship in Latin and in English was small by European standards, the evaluation of Irish materials cited in works in other languages did not stand out as exceptional, regardless of the linguistic and cultural standpoint of the authors.

The earlier works of Charles O'Conor of Belanagare, who had the best understanding of the literary tradition among Irish antiquarians of his century, had little focus on Fionn; his *Dissertations on the Antient History of Ireland* (1753) merely notes 'the standing Army under FIN *Mac* CUMHAL, that excellent Commander and learned Casuist during the reign of Cormac' and that '*Fin Mac Cumhaill*, that King's Son-in-Law, and General of his Army, wrote also on the same Subject [law]'.[9] O'Conor provides neither further discussion of what he regarded as historical, nor any evaluation of the literature. It is clear that the bare annalistic

---

[7] Mac Craith, 'Tadhg Ó Cianáin: Spaghetti *Fiannaigheacht*'. The use of Fenian models for non-Fenian compositions, albeit not for nationalistic reasons, has a longer history; for a medieval example, see Flahive, 'A Hero's Lament'.

[8] '*Fiannaigheacht*, Family, Faith, and Fatherland', 162.

[9] Pp. xxii and 154.

obit of Fionn is the limit of what he is willing to affirm as historical. In the second edition (1766) of his work, O'Conor repeats these remarks with the brief addition that Fionn was 'Chief of the *Basgnean* Clan'.[10] Between these two editions, however, the Ossianic controversies, which will be described in the following chapter, had broken out.

James Macpherson, a Scot, argued for a purely Scottish origin for Fionn and his men, and published what he claimed were English translations of two surviving epics and some fragments concerning them; he also produced a volume which he asserted was a history of Britain and Ireland in the Dark Ages, making use of his literary claims to make Ireland a Scottish colony. O'Conor's second edition therefore defended the learned Irish historical tradition against Macpherson in an additional dissertation of sixty-five pages appended to the revised work. The interest in O'Conor's contribution here is his manner of argument. He treats at considerable length of Macpherson's literary works directly.[11] Within this discussion, O'Conor draws attention to internal inconsistencies in the chronology and genealogy underlying Macpherson.[12] Although he explicitly refers his reader to the excellent article by a 'Sçavant Irlandois' who explores the romances and lays that he demonstrates were in fact Macpherson's sources, O'Conor himself never so much as mentions any Fenian literary text, much less draws on its authority.[13] It is clear that if Keating treated the romances as being an accretion of fable onto history, O'Conor, who knew the learned tradition better than anyone from his time until the advent of the scholars of the late nineteenth and early twentieth centuries, would not taint his history with the names of such texts. Nevertheless, his affirmation of the historical position of Fionn and his men was more forceful than his rejection of the value of the literature to the historian.

The consensus position of the nineteenth century grew from this tradition; it could vary from a vague distrust like O'Conor's to

---

[10] O'Conor, *A Dissertation on the First Migrations*, 17.

[11] Ibid., 22–34.

[12] For example, his analysis of the mix-up of Fenian and Ultonian characters presented as contemporary (p. 27), and the historical setting that conflates into Macpherson's tale characters as chronologically removed as the Roman emperor Caracalla and Lochlannaigh from Viking raids of the ninth century (pp. 39–41).

[13] Ibid., 63; see Sçavant Irlandois, 'Mémoire de M. de C. à Messieurs les Auteurs du Journal des Sçavans, au sujet des poëmes de M. Macpherson'. Thanks are due to Diarmaid Ó Catháin for bringing this extremely rare publication to the author's attention and for furnishing a copy of it for this study.

a desire to extract as much for history as possible as Keating had done. The enthusiasm for the latter end of this scale was by far the greater in Ireland, where defence of the antiquity of the national tradition was seen as a patriotic duty. Figures such as Owen Connellan provided more vehement, nationalistic, anti-Scottish scholarly contributions of this type.[14]

O'Curry's *Lectures on the Manuscript Materials of Ancient Irish History* (1861) provided the first scholarly evaluation of the Irish manuscript corpus with a view to the writing of accurate histories that took Irish-language sources into account, something which had been altogether lacking at the time (1855–6) he delivered the lectures. O'Curry confines his treatment of the Fenian Cycle, occasional mentions in passing aside, to the chapter titled 'Of the Imaginative Tales and Poems',[15] and a small section on prophecies attributed to Fionn.[16] He draws attention to the value of the tales as a record of the customs and toponyms at the time when they were written.[17] O'Curry cites O'Conor (and his antiquarian grandson of the same name) on the bare facts, but also uses the genealogical tradition, especially from LL, to add weight to the antiquity and learnedness of the tradition. His belief, however, stretches further; he is pleased to find five poems between LL and the Book of Lecan (RIA MS 23 P 2 [535]) attributed to Fionn that he could 'ascribe [to him], upon anything like respectable authority', though he proceeds to question one of these, before giving two additional items as possibly authentic.[18] From the chronicles, genealogies, and potentially truly ancient poems, O'Curry distinguishes a small number of Middle Irish poems that he thinks may have some slight historical foundation; and then sequesters the later poems and romances, which he considers purely creative literature, yet valuable as sources for later cultural details. His treatment of the Fenian Cycle was more generous than O'Conor's austere reserve, but more restrained than Keating's enthusiastic use of the tales. He summarises his position:

> I may, however, take occasion to assure you that it is quite a mistake to suppose *Finn Mac Cumhaill* to have been a merely imaginary or mythical character. Much that has been narrated

---

[14] 'The poems of Ossian by Macpherson' directly followed by 'On the Fians of Erin and the Poems of Oisin, the Celebrated Bard'.

[15] Lecture xiv, 296–319.

[16] Ibid., lecture xix, 392–6.

[17] Ibid., 298.

[18] Ibid., 300–4 at 302.

of his exploits is, no doubt, apocryphal enough; but Finn himself is an undoubtedly historical personage; and that he existed about the time at which his appearance is recorded in the annals, is as certain as that Julius Caesar lived and ruled at the time stated on the authority of the Roman historians.[19]

For decades, scholarship followed O'Curry's lead; the next attempt to survey the literature comprehensively, undertaken by Henri d'Arbois de Jubainville, used *Leabhar Gabhála*, the chronicles, and other sources for a chronology of the cycle. Like O'Conor, he sought an historical core behind the literature, but kept this search wholly separate from his literary analysis of the later texts.[20]

Challenges to the consensus began to appear in the nineteenth century. W.F. Skene took a critical view of the Irish historical record of the annals and medieval pseudo-histories as early as 1862. He proceeded to analyse the position of the Fenians in depth as part of his introduction to Thomas M'Lauchlan's edition of the poems in BDL. Skene thought that the *fiana* emerged 'from under the guise of a Milesian militia' to 'assume the features of a distinct race', which he identified as remnants of Fir Bholg and other, possibly also Brittonic, subject peoples.[21] He concluded that the tradition therefore had to be even older than the dates in Irish chronicles suggested, and that it had localised itself in both Scotland and Ireland over centuries. In the first volume of *DF*, published in 1904, Eoin MacNeill proposed a related theory that adopted Skene's racial argument, but accepted the traditional chronology. He proposed that the *fiana* were armies created in imitation of the Roman legions present in Britain from the first to early fifth centuries, but which largely consisted of the men of subject Fir Bholg peoples held in military servitude by their Milesian Gaelic overlords. He read the struggle between Clann Bhaoiscne and Clann Mhorna as reflecting a conflict between the Gáileóin, a people of South Leinster, and Fir Bholg of Connaught.[22] The recruitment of subject peoples as troops was by no means unfamiliar in MacNeill's Ireland and provided him with inspiration, but the British Empire mainly used its Irish and Scottish regiments

---

[19] Ibid., 303–4.

[20] *Cours de la Littérature Celtique*, v, 375–8.

[21] *The Dean of Lismore's Book*, pp. lxiv–lxxxiii at p. lxxii. The Milesians are the Gaelic people, and Fir Bholg are generally understood to be one of the peoples previously established in Ireland. Their Celticity (like their historicity) is a matter of scholarly debate.

[22] *DF* i, pp. xxiv–lii.

abroad to combat external threats in India, Jamaica, and other far-away lands: a trained, armed — and rebellious — subject people, based at home, is unlikely to remain as long in servitude as MacNeill's theory requires.[23]

The second new approach to appear was Heinrich Zimmer's theory of Hiberno-Norse origins. Zimmer, who held fanatical beliefs about Germanic ethnic superiority, believed that Irish and Celtic literature in general could not have flourished without the infusion of the Germanic Norse genius. The foundations of the theory first appeared in 1887 in a very critical review of d'Arbois de Jubainville's *Essai d'un catalogue de la littérature épique de l'Irlande*. Zimmer proposed that Fionn was based on an historical Dublin Viking, Ketil Hvíte, Gaelicised as Caittil Find; he furthermore identified supposed Norse origins for the names Oisín and Oscar.[24] Although his theory entered into popular consciousness and controversy, other scholars were doubtful. Responses, however, focused on the inaccuracy of Zimmer's transcriptions and translations in a number of publications that addressed his broader theory, much of which extends beyond the Fenian Cycle.[25] Among the scholars engaged in the debate, only Alfred Nutt took on his full arguments directly. Nutt first responded in a review of recent scholarship on Celtic literature in 1888, where he touched on a number of Zimmer's publications, holding that '[i]t is somewhat difficult to keep one's countenance over this amazing instance of perverted ingenuity'; Nutt later revisited the subject, still sceptically, in a brief article reviewing Zimmer's revised and expanded theory in 'Keltische Beiträge'.[26] Having received a personal response from Zimmer, he printed the corrections provided as a continuation in the next fascicle of the volume. He then proceeded to make his reservations more explicit by expressing relief at Whitley Stokes' philological undercutting of Zimmer's posited Norse etymologies for the names of the *féinnidhthe*; Nutt regarded Stokes' comments as pulling the rug out from under the theory and rendering the need for a more considered response based in literary criticism unnecessary.[27]

---

[23] Flahive, 'The Relic Lays', 64–5.

[24] 'Keltische Beiträge III'; 'Ossin und Oskar'.

[25] Stokes, 'Zimmeriana', 97–100; Meyer, Review of Zimmer, 'Keltische Beiträge I'; d'Arbois de Jubainville, Review of Zimmer, 'Keltische Beiträge III'.

[26] Nutt, 'Celtic Myth and Saga', 141; 'A New Theory of Ossianic Saga'.

[27] Nutt, 'A New Theory of Ossianic Saga', 235.

A competing view of the nature of the Fenians was that Fionn was absolutely ahistorical and of mythological origins. Its seed may be found in the Presbyterian dismissal of Fionn in John Carswell's address to the reader that accompanies his 1567 translation of the Church of Scotland's *Book of Common Order*.[28] This negative rhetoric placed Fionn outside the human world in mythological company, while at the same time dismissing the tales as lying and foolish:

> eachtradha dímhaoineacha buaidheartha brégacha saoghalta, do cumadh ar Thuathaibh Dé Dhanond, agas ar Mhacaibh Míleadh, agas ar na curadhaibh, agas ar Fhind mhac Cumhaill gona Fhianaibh, agas móran eile nach áirbhim ...[29]

> unprofitable, annoying, lying, worldly adventures that were composed about the Tuatha Dé Danann, and the Sons of Míl, and about the heroes, and about Fionn mac Cumhaill with his Fiana, and many more that I cannot count ...

Carswell was clearly employing hyperbolic language to contrast the traditional tales concerning Finn with the study of Scripture. Behind this view there seems to be a position, not so far from that of Keating, that the romances and adventures were exactly that. What historical fragments were generally believed to underlie them were not actually denied; they were simply not of interest to Carswell. The opposition of lying stories and Gospel Truth, unprofitable distractions versus Scripture, and fleeting worldly temptations against the eternal joys of heaven: these are the focus of his arguments. Nevertheless, if these characters are seen as non-Christian and the tales false and worthless in the view of a reforming cleric — and of many who followed after him — nevertheless, he had taken steps towards classification of the Fenian Cycle as both pagan and ahistorical.

The first scholar to suggest a mythological Fionn explicitly was J.F. Campbell. He interpreted the folklore of the Highlands that he collected as the remnant of pre-Christian mythology and culture, placing it in the context of the emerging comparative study of Indo-European cultures, with a heavy reliance on the then-fashionable solar divinity theory.[30] He argues that since

---

[28] Ed. with commentary by R.L. Thomson, *Foirm na n-Urrnuidheadh*.

[29] Ibid. 11, ll. 324–7.

[30] See *Popular Tales of the West Highlands*, 2nd ed., iv, Chapter Three.

'Villemarque holds that Arthur and his knights are but Celtic gods in disguise, surely the Fenians are but another phase of the same astronomical worship of the host of heaven'.[31] Campbell's line of thought had only a few followers in the nineteenth century, most of them in Britain; the re-assertion of the traditional view of a vaguely historical Fionn lying behind the legends found a strong champion in Eugene O'Curry, Campbell's Irish contemporary. The scholarly consensus following O'Curry continued through the early twentieth century, until the mythological Fionn in time came into general acceptance after the publication of T.F. O'Rahilly's *Early Irish History and Mythology* and Murphy's introduction to *DF* iii (as described in Chapter Two above).

Nevertheless, at the close of the nineteenth century and into the first decade of the twentieth century — even among the first rank of scholars — the consensus of an historical basis generally held, but most ceased to argue seriously about the origins of the Fenian legends, being content to focus on them as literature. As philology progressively revealed the age of early Irish texts more accurately, more doubts were entertained, but at that time there did not appear to be much intellectual profit in exploring them when the task at hand was to edit and to analyse medieval literature of many centuries later. Thus L.C. Stern produced a sixty-eight-page analysis of the ballad tradition and its background that treated possible origins in a single paragraph in which he mentioned challenges to the historicity of the Ulster Cycle and Zimmer's theory in a solitary sentence. He then moved on to describe the matter as buried in 'primaeval myth' before dropping the issue and proceeding directly to discuss the texts.[32] Kuno Meyer similarly tiptoed around discussing origins in his introduction to *Fianaig-echt*, wherein he listed and evaluated the corpus of texts up to the fourteenth century; nevertheless, he was happy enough to draw attention (p. 15) to legendary accretion within the literature.

Alfred Nutt's views of the lays and romances, which he expounded at greater length, are typical of later Victorian understanding and its rather more sceptical approach:

> we may disregard the otherwise interesting question of historic credibility in the Ossianic romances: firstly, because they have their being in a land unaffected by fact; secondly, because if they ever did reflect the history of the third century, the reflection

---

[31] Ibid., iv, 293.
[32] 'Ossianic Heroic Poetry', 287.

was distorted in after-times, and a pseudo-history based upon events of the ninth and tenth centuries was substituted for it.[33]

Nutt was just barely a believer in an historical Fionn; he allowed for a grain of truth, like the sand at the centre of a pearl:

> I assumed, in common with all previous investigation, and in accordance with the apparent meaning of the earliest Irish records, that it was furnished by the life and deeds of a third-century Irishman, Finn son of Cumhal. At the same time, I expressed the opinion that the historical elements in the cycle were of little importance in comparison to the romantic ones.[34]

He questioned the extent to which early Irish history incorporated mythological and pseudo-historical elements (versus truly historical ones) as, by the end of the nineteenth century, scholarship had come to understand that the process of compiling the early medieval chronicle materials was non-contemporary. He hinted at seeing the shadows of tribal deities in proto-historical figures, but he did not labour the point.[35] According to Nutt, no identifiable residue of an historical Fionn could be found in a literary 'fairyland' intermixed with fictionalised Viking raids.[36] These later views continued to hold.

In many households of Ireland or Gaelic Scotland, the tales were still told by the fireside and the lays chanted into the twentieth century, without concern for the theories of antiquarians or historians. It is only the accelerated weakening of the living tradition since the mid-nineteenth century that has brought an increasingly independent scholarly strand to the fore; this has happened at the same time as the Fenian Cycle's connection with the now-extinct native learned tradition has atrophied.

---

[33] Nutt, *Ossian and the Ossianic Literature*, 2nd ed., 11.

[34] 'Introduction' to MacDougall, *Folk and Hero Tales*, p. xxii. This statement is his own summary of 'Development of the Fenian or Ossianic Saga', published in MacInnes, *Folk and Hero Tales*, 399–430; see the diagram on p. 417 for his account of the evolution of the saga from its sources. Nutt restated this position in 'A New Theory of the Ossianic Saga', 161.

[35] See his introduction to Campbell, *The Fians*, pp. xiv–xxi; MacInnes, *Folk and Hero Tales*, 409–10. Notably, however, incorrect claims that Nutt held the position of a purely mythological origin have been made by a number of scholars (for example, Curteis, 'Age and Origin of the Fenian Tales', 164; MacLean, *The Literature of the Celt*, 175).

[36] Nutt, *Ossian and the Ossianic Literature*, 2nd ed., 53–4. He follows with a direct rebuttal of MacNeill, 55–9.

7. The Long Twilight

Two eighteenth-century Irish lays, '*Laoidh Cholainn gan Chionn*' and '*Laoidh Oisín ar Thír na nÓg*', explain Oisín's extraordinary survival into the fifth century.[1] A third lay, '*Lá dhúinne ar Sliabh Fuaid*' ('One day as we were on Slieve Fuaid'), was also composed in the eighteenth century, possibly by Muiris Ó Gormáin.[2] Máire Ní Mhuirgheasa dated the romances edited in *Sgéalta Rómánsuíochta*, of which *Eachtra Thailc Mhic Thréun* was the only Fenian text, to the end of the seventeenth century. Although other romances without firmly assigned dates may be as late, none have been identified as likely to have been composed after the early eighteenth century. At that point, the long-dominant form of the romance ceased to be an active model for constructing prose narratives. As the lay and the romance faded away, literary *fianaigheacht* gradually ceased to be productive in the Irish tradition by the mid-eighteenth century.[3] Throughout the nineteenth century, the lays and Early Modern romances were widely copied and circulated in manuscript, but that century elapsed without significant addition to the corpus. Because copies were frequently read aloud, many stories passed from written sources into folk tradition. Oral variants of many of them have since been collected. In time, the living tradition also came to suffer with the widespread decline of the Irish language. The last official collection of lays recorded from the living tradition in Ireland was in 1959.[4] This is the point at which scholarship considered that all the material had been collected; it is not the point at which traditional performance ceased.[5] Nevertheless, the living memory of these poems outside scholarly editions and learned revival was hanging by a thread by 1950, and it appears that the final diminuendo of the voice of inherited literary *fianaigheacht* is now complete. In contrast, the Fenian folktale lives and even remains productive, more than a

---

[1] See above p. 7, n. 26.

[2] Ó Dubhthaigh, 'Agallamh Oisín agus Phádraig: "Lá dhúinne ar Sliabh Fuaid"', 35.

[3] See Breatnach, 'The End of a Tradition'.

[4] Ó Baoighill, *Amhráin Hiúdaí Fheilimí agus Laoithe Fiannaíochta*, 67.

[5] It is certain that the tradition lingered as long elsewhere, with or without magnetic tape to preserve it; for example, Alan Titley informs me that he heard lays performed in An Fheothanach, Co. Kerry in June 1963, though he does not know the name of the *seanchaidh*.

generation later.[6]

In Gaelic Scotland, however, the tradition has faded somewhat more slowly. A mixed blessing came in the middle of the eighteenth century when James Macpherson, a Highland Gael with knowledge of the tradition, published loose translations — or rather adaptations — of several lays and prose tales, which were presented as though verse in prose translation, *Fragments of Ancient Poetry* (1760). Finding these well received, he proceeded to create two epics, *Fingal* (1761) and *Temora* (1763), both accompanied by a number of shorter pieces, written in English rhetorical prose, though he attached a Gaelic version of book VII of *Temora* (which is now generally considered at least in part to be the work of a kinsman, Lachlan Macpherson, based on the testimony of the *Report of the Highland Society*).[7] Macpherson's works claimed to be translations of Gaelic works of the third century, composed by Ossian (his Anglicisation of Oisín, via the Scots-Gaelic form Oisean), but were in fact based on retellings of lays and Fenian romances, strung together with materials of his own invention, and recentred on the Scottish Highlands.[8] Over the course of his activity, his works departed more and more from their models, and *Temora* is generally agreed to be his own invention, apart from a few scenes.

Macpherson's Ossian, as the works came to be called, proved a literary sensation across Europe, with hundreds of editions and translations into almost every European language, but their authenticity soon came to be doubted by many. The Ossianic contro-

---

[6] Mention must be made here of the Fenian folklore catalogue (containing metadata for over 3,000 folklore items) created by Natasha Sumner which was submitted as a supplement to her Harvard doctoral dissertation in 2015. She intends to use this catalogue in coming years to underpin an online Fenian folklore database project.

[7] There is a handlist of the original editions of Macpherson's works provided by Gaskill in his introduction to *Ossian Revisited*, 2–3; Stafford, *The Sublime Savage*, 185–7, includes the listing of his non-Ossianic works. Moore, *Ossian and Ossianism*, is a facsimile collection in four volumes, presenting the first editions of all Macpherson's works, accompanied by many rare eighteenth-century works bearing on the controversy (some of which print specimens of authentic lays and other materials of use for the study of *fianaigheacht*). The standard reference edition of Ossian is that of Gaskill (ed.), *The Poems of Ossian and Related Works*. For additional bibliography of editions, see below n. 11.

[8] Ronald Black provides a handlist of the accessible Gaelic written sources, 'Surviving Gaelic Manuscripts Collected by James Macpherson', published in Stafford, *The Sublime Savage*, 148.

versies, as they came to be known, drew in many of the figures of the British literary and intellectual world, including such men as Samuel Johnson, David Hume, Hugh Blair, and even Charles O'Conor.[9] The question grew more complicated when a full Gaelic version of Macpherson's compositions was published post-humously in 1807.[10] This version has since been demonstrated to have been translated from the English, but it claimed to be the ancient original, although it was written in modern Scots Gaelic (like the *Temora* segment printed with the first English edition), with the idiomatic savour of Macpherson's English style carried through rather than the traditional style of the Fenian lays. By this time, both James and Lachlan Macpherson were dead, and others quietly carried on the fabrication for more than a decade after the originators were gone. Debate on the authenticity of Ossian continued through much of the nineteenth century until scholarship came to understand the evolution of the Gaelic languages; the question of the extent to which the work represented traditional materials and texts as opposed to Macpherson's own compositions was not resolved definitively until 1952.[11]

Macpherson's works, however, cannot be regarded as *fianaigheacht*. His compositions do not fit into the cycle; rather, they re-imagine it.[12] His characters supposedly inhabit the third century, but encounter characters from other periods and literary cycles, most especially heroes and plots from the Ulster Cycle, which are

---

[9] For a recent account of the early stages of the controversy with focus on Johnson, see Curley, *Samuel Johnson, the Ossian Fraud, and the Celtic Revival in Great Britain and Ireland*.

[10] Highland Society of London, *The Poems of Ossian, in the Original Gaelic*.

[11] Thomson, *The Gaelic Sources of Macpherson's 'Ossian'*; idem, 'Macpherson's *Ossian*: Ballads to Epics'. Thomson's studies, however, concern only poetic sources, and suggestions that plots were also borrowed from romances are not investigated therein. Although Thomson has established the nature of Macpherson's compositions beyond all doubt, the question of possible prose sources requires further investigation. A different approach, exploring how Macpherson used and was inspired by Gaelic tradition in Ossian, is provided by Mac Craith, 'The "Forging" of Ossian'. The vast quantities of ink spilt on the way to the conclusion may be best appreciated by reference to Black, *Macpherson's Ossian and the Ossianic Controversy: A Contribution Towards a Bibliography*, a pamphlet of forty-one pages of small footnote-sized type in double columns, including full references for editions of Macpherson's works. Black's work, published in 1926, is supplemented and brought up to 1971 by Dunn, 'Macpherson's Ossian and the Ossianic Controversy: A Supplementary Bibliography'.

[12] See Nagy, 'Observations on the Ossianesque'.

admixed with no regard for the tradition. The main action has been transposed to the Scottish Highlands, with Irish places in the poems and tales transformed or eliminated. The traditional Gaelic worldview is gone, replaced by a world of portent, prophecy, wild storms and wastelands, and ghosts. These serve to magnify the purple-prose descriptions that overwhelm the action: the antithesis of the direct, concrete style of Fenian lays. The characters themselves are changed, and no longer fill their traditional roles. Fionn becomes Fingal, king of Scotland; Cú Chulainn becomes his Irish counterpart on the throne. Others become less recognisable still. The world of Ossian is a study in itself, but for most of a century, it entwined itself firmly with *fianaigheacht* in the perception of the Anglophone world and far beyond.

From the interest that Macpherson had stirred, a number of other works of varying types arose. The Ossianic ballads, as the lays were then known, were the chief focus of early study. Two Irish bishops were among the first to bring serious academic rigour to a debate that featured as much mud slinging as argument. An anonymous 'Sçavant Irlandois' (thought to be John O'Brien, the Catholic Bishop of Cork and Cloyne, living in exile in Paris, where he also published an Irish-English dictionary) wrote a reasoned historical analysis of Macpherson's Ossian, which he compared to *Leabhar Gabhála* ('The Book of Invasions'), genealogies, chronicles, and Latin histories.[13] This article presents the first modern scholarship on the Fenian Cycle, and the last instalment of it contains a discussion of a number of the romances and lays, including '*Laoidh an Deirg*', *Bruidhean Chaorthainn*, and *Cath Fionntrágha*, as well as the Early Modern recension of the Ulster-Cycle tale *Oidheadh Chloinne hUisneach* ('The Violent Death of the Children of Uisneach'), from which O'Brien demonstrated that Macpherson had borrowed.[14] No scholar has investigated the relationship between prose romances and Ossian in depth in more than two centuries since. Matthew Young (the mathematician and scholar who later served the Church of Ireland as bishop of Clonfert and Kilmacduagh) travelled from Ireland to the Scottish Highlands in 1784 to ascertain the extent of the Fenian tradition there; he printed a substantial collection of lays, some of which were transcribed from oral recitation rather than copied from manuscripts.[15] Other collections were gathered and

---

[13] 'Mémoire de M. de C.'.

[14] Ibid., 845–54.

[15] Young, 'Antient Gaelic Poems Respecting the Race of the Fians'.

published quite rapidly in both Ireland and Scotland.[16] The texts in such collections recorded the breakdown of the Early Modern literary standard and the assimilation of the poetry into the dialects of the areas where they were collected. Nevertheless, the collectors uncovered a rich body of additional ballads, variant versions, and fragments. The Ossianic controversies drew attention to the Fenian Cycle — and indeed to literature in the Gaelic languages in general — throughout Europe. This in turn contributed to the wider recognition that the Gaelic languages were worthy of serious academic study.

Broader culture embraced the sensation. Beyond the academy, during the height of its popularity, Ossian not only sat on Napoleon's bedside table but influenced the German 'Sturm und Drang' movement and Romantic poets such as Herder and Schiller.

---

[16] Only one collection of Fenian lays taken from oral sources rather than manuscripts predates Macpherson's publications. This is found in two notebooks of Jerome Stone, a Fife schoolmaster, who recorded them in the mideighteenth century; both volumes are now in Edinburgh, University Library MSS La.3.251 (Laing 251) and La.3.251*. The collection is printed by MacKinnon, 'Collection of Ossianic Ballads by Jerome Stone'. Post-Macpherson collections, on the other hand, are numerous: in 1782–3, Hill published 'New Lights on the Ossian Controversy' as a series of short items in *Gentleman's Magazine*, later reprinted (1784) in a pamphlet, *Antient Erse Poems*. Gillies, *A Collection of Ancient and Modern Gaelic Poems and Songs*, contains a number of ballad texts from various sources among its songs and poems, including authentic materials, with many items apparently printed from Stone's collections. Gaelic verse translations from Macpherson's *Ossian*, and a fragment called 'Mordubh' based on an anonymous English piece called 'Morduth', were published by John Clark (see Thomson, 'Some Bogus Gaelic Literature', esp. 178–82). Another collection of authentic materials made in 1805 has been printed and discussed by Cameron, 'Poems of Ossian Collected by John McDonald'. In Ireland, the great milestone in publishing the lays was Charlotte Brooke, *Reliques of Irish Poetry*. Spurred on by Macpherson's claim that Fenian literature was distinctly Scottish, she published and translated a miscellany of lays and other verse from manuscripts in the Royal Irish Academy; and the Irish originals contained in that work constitute the first literary work presented using Irish type to be printed in Ireland, all previous publications having been produced abroad and imported. Although long forgotten, the work of Charles Wilson, who published a number of lays and poems in translation, some accompanied by the Irish originals printed in Roman type, preceded Brooke with his first collection, *Poems Translated from the Irish Language into the English*, and followed with another, the anonymously published *Select Irish Poems*. His work has been re-evaluated by Mac Craith in 'Charles Wilson (*c.* 1756–1808): Réamhtheachtaí Charlotte Brooke' and '"We Know All These Poems": The Irish Response to *Ossian*'.

Goethe wove Ossian deeply into the climax of *Die Leiden des junges Werther*; this scene in turn inspired the aria 'Pourquoi me réveiller?' in Massenet's operatic adaptation 'Werther'. Ossianism further presented itself as a theme in other arts, such as the Classicised vision presented in paintings such Jean Auguste-Dominique Ingres' 'The Dream of Ossian'. In music, Beethoven's attention was drawn by the Ossianic idea of the bard; he arranged multiple Irish and Scottish airs as *Lieder*, and Mendelsson also drew inspiration from Ossian for symphonic works such as 'The Hebrides Overture' (also known as 'Fingal's Cave').[17] The *fiana* arrived at the opera in 'Ossian ou Les Bardes' by Le Sueur.

The antiquarians and amateur scholars who engaged in a fierce debate about Ossian were not alone in providing literary responses to the wider cultural phenomenon. Duncan Kennedy and the Rev. John Smith of Campbelltown took another tack altogether.[18] Kennedy's manuscript collections included authentic traditional material alongside creative adaptations of traditional lays, in which he made the tone more like Macpherson's, eliminating Irish place-names in favour of Scottish ones, inserting stanzas of his own creation, trying his hand at compositions in the lay form as well; fundamentally, however, his texts fit into the world of traditional *fianaigheacht*, more than the new composite of Macpherson's *Fingal*. His collections were not published in full until long after his death.[19] After two centuries of near total neglect, Anja Gunderloch has begun to re-assess them, and has drawn renewed attention to the fact that Smith borrowed one of Kennedy's notebooks; testimony of this loan was made to and published by the Highland Society's committee on the authenticity of Ossian. Smith is likely to have recognised Kennedy's alterations to the widely circulating traditional versions and to have drawn his own inspiration from them.[20] The Rev. Smith was the more creative of the two; he published lays in both Gaelic and in English translation, a number of which — such as his '*Laoidh an Deirg*' ('Lay

---

[17] Gaskill, *The Reception of Ossian in Europe*, collects many valuable papers on the translations of Ossian and their widespread influence in European literature.

[18] General observations on Smith and Kennedy comprise a substantial portion of Thomson's essay 'Some Bogus Gaelic Literature'.

[19] The original collections are NLS Adv. MS 72.3.9 (Gaelic MS LXXXVII) and Adv. MS 72.3.10 (Gaelic MS XXXVIII). Kennedy's compilations are printed in Campbell, *Leabhar na Feinne*, as collections H and L.

[20] Mackenzie, *Report of the Highland Society*, 107–9; Gunderloch, 'Duncan Kennedy and his Heroic Ballads'.

of the Red-Haired Man') — appear to be entirely of his own creation.[21] As a minister, he held not only the high degree of Scots-Gaelic literacy necessary to compose sermons for his Gaelic-speaking parish, but he was one of the team of translators who worked on the first Scots-Gaelic Old Testament. Many Scottish churches used a Roman-type edition of William Bedell's seventeenth-century Irish translation, and the project in which Smith was employed involved extensive consultation with it, providing direct evidence of Smith's professional familiarity with Early Modern Irish. Smith's versifying abilities are also on display in his hymnal; this contains translations into Gaelic (not always acknowledged as such) alongside hymns of his own composition; it was reprinted multiple times throughout the nineteenth century.[22] It is difficult to know whether it would be more accurate to credit Smith as one of the last composers of lays — and a rather prolific one at that — or whether he should be dismissed like Macpherson with terms like 'fraud' or 'impostor' for his claim to be printing old poems. He certainly taunted his readers, and this may have ultimately diminished his reputation, as Thomson observes:

> Frequently, in a note on a particular line or passage, he gives an alternative reading — both readings being spurious ... He sometimes refers to passages from genuine ballads, sometimes quoting these, only to discredit them as 'ur-sgeuls' or 'later tales' ... His cool impudence is admirable.[23]

Smith's works borrowed much of the setting and framework of Macpherson's plots, even if they drew in other ways on the authentic tradition, taking in parts of lays from Kennedy's collection and possibly from other poems that he knew, along with plots from romances. Although Macpherson was a Gael, he was not very literate in his native tongue; he probably composed in English and required helpers to provide a Gaelic version or at least to transcribe and to polish it, when it was demanded; Smith, on the other hand, was a well-known writer who composed readily in his native language, yet he chose to adopt Macpherson's storm-and-stress style of composition and some elements from the world of Mac-

---

[21] These were printed in two collections, one English and one Gaelic: Smith, *Galic Antiquities*; idem, *Sean Dana*. A school edition of two of Smith's poems (with normalised spellings and new English versions) was edited by Jerram, *Dàn an Deirg, agus Tiomna Ghuill*.

[22] *Urnaighean arson Theaghlaichean, &c, agus Laoidhean.*

[23] 'Some Bogus Gaelic Literature', 180.

pherson's heroic pastiche, which had no antecedents in the tradition, rather than work within the more authentic world of the *fiana* that Smith knew well. On the other hand, he did not tolerate the Ulster-Cycle intrusions or a number of similar departures from *fianaigheacht* introduced in the world of Macpherson's Ossianic Cycle. Amusingly, in English, Smith's bombastic prose proved so over-the-top that Charles Jerram provided new translations on the grounds that Smith could not do (his own) Gaelic justice.[24] Had he lived a generation earlier, scholars might well have celebrated him as a major poet for bringing early Romanticism into Gaelic. Smith created something new in Gaelic literature, but in the end, the question as to whether his works are *fianaigheacht* is moot. Thomson, coming down against, spoke thus: 'There seem to have been two main schools of fabricated Ossianic verse: a Badenoch one and a Glenorchy one, the latter composing first in Gaelic and then translating into English'.[25] Elsewhere he asserts that 'the opposite is generally the case with the Badenoch school' of which Macpherson was the chief member.[26] Thomson did not approve of this sort of literature at all, writing of 'the vicious effects of the "Ossianic" style'.[27] In the other camp, Jerram was its chief Victorian enthusiast.[28] Perhaps it is best to let the reader judge. The materials could be heroic verse:

Bhuail mac Morn' an t-ath-bheum sgéithe;
(Cha b'ionann a h-éigh a's an tràsa) —
Chlisg an I, a's dhùisg a cathan;
Dhùldaich Goll, 's lann athar a' dealradh*
   *Al. — Bhuail iad mar thein-adhair thun tràgha.

Gach taobh dheth tha daoine 'g an sgathadh,
Mar ùr-bharrach an doire na fàsaich;
An airm lìomhaidh 's an raon air an sgapadh,
'S eoin na h-ealtainn ri gàire.[29]

Jerram provides a literal translation:

[24] *Dàn an Deirg agus Tiomna Ghuill*, p. viii.
[25] Thomson, 'From Gaelic to Romantic', 26.
[26] Thomson, 'Some Bogus Gaelic Literature', 185.
[27] Ibid., 188.
[28] Jerram, 'Some Causes of the Imperfect Appreciation by Englishmen of the Ossianic Poems'.
[29] Jerram, *Dàn an Deirg agus Tiomna Ghuill*, 58.

Morni's son smote the shield again;
(Not then as at this day was its sound) —
The isle started; the men of war awoke;
Dark was Gaul's frown — bright flashed the brand of his
    sire.*
    *Al. — They rushed like lightning to the shore.

On every side he hewed down the men,
Like green branches in the moorland grove;
Their polished arms are strewn upon the plain,
And flocking birds exultant laugh around.[30]

Smith himself was rather more florid, and his translation departs from his text:

The shield of Morni is struck again in Ifrona. No half-consumed, earth-crusted board was this orb then! Ifrona rocked with its sound, and its thousands gathered around Gaul. But the sword of Morni is in the terrible hand of the chief; and, like the green branches of the forest, their ranks are hewn before him. Their blue arms are strewed upon the heath, and the birds of death are hovering round.[31]

Yet Smith could write quatrains in the same poem of a romantic character quite alien to the tradition:

'S bha 'n oidhche doilleir duaichnidh;
Torman speur mar chreig romh sgàrnaich;
Uillt a' beucaich, — taibhs' a' sgreadail;
'S boisgeadh tein' o'n adhar bholg-dhubh.[32]

Dark and dismal was the night;
The sky murmured like rending rocks;
Loud roared the torrents, — shrieked the ghosts;
Lightnings flashed from heaven's dark dome.[33]

The night was stormy and dark: ghosts shrieked on the heath: torrents roared from the rock of the hill: thunders

---

[30] Ibid., 59.
[31] Smith, *Galic Antiquities*, 158–9.
[32] Jerram, *Dàn an Deirg agus Tiomna Ghuill*, 48.
[33] Ibid., 49.

roared like breaking rocks, through clouds, and lightnings
travelled on their dark-red wings through the sky.[34]

Has Smith out-Macphersoned Macpherson?

Another prominent early collection (1816) is Hugh and John
M'Callum, *An Original Collection of the Poems of Ossian, Orran,
Ulin, and Other Bards.* There are in fact two books here: one of
the Gaelic texts (exceedingly rare) and one of English translations
(very common), both of which have the same English title-page,
which is a cause of some confusion. This book muddies the
waters, crossing the line from Ossianism to *fianaigheacht* and
back again multiple times. It prints a number of traditional lays,
but mixes in two of Smith's compositions (disguised by using the
names of friends of his as 'sources'). It also presents other passages of doubtful origins employing a similar style (all supplied
by ministers of the church), as well as the popular passage
'Ossian's Address to the Rising Sun' from the Gaelic edition of
Macpherson.[35] Smith, if the most prolific, was not the only imita-
tor of Macpherson in Gaelic, not to mention English.[36]

Scotland's tradition received a great boon from many more
of her ministers and from a number of other scholars who published transcripts of folktales. As Bruford has established in *Gaelic
Folk-tales and Mediaeval Romances,* these folktales are frequently the descendants of the romances, and are often not far
removed from links to the manuscript tradition; of these tales,
those belonging to the Fenian Cycle garnered the most attention
due to the influence of Ossianism. Though most of these men
attempted to be as accurate as possible, the work of transcribing a
story from recitation in the days of goose quills and inkpots rather
than electric recording devices necessitated a slow, painstaking
telling and revision in the course of several repetitions of the tale.
Furthermore, one may expect that the ministers, educated as they
were in the Gaelic rhetoric of the pulpit, were not always entirely
silent transcribers, regardless of their intentions, and certainly

---

[34] Smith, *Galic Antiquities,* 154.

[35] Thomson, 'Some Bogus Gaelic Literature', 183–7.

[36] A curious item, perhaps worthy of citation to demonstrate the sheer extent
of Ossianism, is the Limerick-born Baron von Harold's 1775 translation of
Macpherson, *Die Gedichte Ossian's* [sic] *eines alten celtischen Helden und
Barden,* in which he forged in German three 'newly found' additional
poems, 'Bosmina', 'Ossians letzes Lied', and 'Ossians Lied nach der Römer
Niederlage' (iii, 235–62). For an account of his life and activity, see Ó
Catháin, 'General Baron Edmond Harold'.

exercised their judgement in the transition from first draft to fair copy. It is unsurprising that these folktales, as they appear in print, have an elegance and polish that is lacking in non-professional manuscripts or later audio recordings of traditional storytelling; yet it is readily apparent that these collectors did not impart an inauthentic or unnatural style to them because their literary judgements stood within the living tradition of which they were members.[37] If the stories were not new, the prose style in which they have been preserved in such collections as *The Fians* and *Popular Tales of the West Highlands* has proven a worthy successor to the bombastic adjective-laden alliterative prose of so many late romances; indeed, generations of students of Scots Gaelic have turned to them for their elegant simplicity.[38] Alongside these prose collections, there were attempts to preserve the lays; hundreds were taken down or (in later times) recorded, and most have been printed.[39] The attention that the lays received from scholarship from an early date helped to re-enforce the tradition in Gaelic Scotland, where the chanting of Fenian lays lives yet.

---

[37] Compare the attitude of Gerard Murphy to the process of transcribing (*Saga and Myth in Ancient Ireland*, 10–11), where, following an anecdote about Domhnall Bán Ó Céileachair writing, narrating, and revising his autobiography, he opines, '[w]hen, therefore, we form a picture of the orally narrated Irish tale as something immeasurably superior to the suggestions of it a monastic scribe has recorded, we are not creating a figment of the imagination, we are merely restoring to the corpse buried in a manuscript the soul that once animated it'.

[38] J.F. Campbell, *Popular Tales of the West Highlands*; J.G. Campbell, *The Fians*.

[39] J.F. Campbell's *Leabhar na Feinne* is the largest collection; he lists earlier publications in his introduction. Mention must also be made of the McLagan collection in Glasgow University Library, containing more than two hundred manuscripts, from which only selections have been published. A catalogue of ninety-five Fenian lays in the collection is found in Thomson, 'A Catalogue and Indexes of the Ossianic Ballads in the McLagan MSS'. The compilations of a number of further nineteenth-century collectors are preserved in the manuscript holdings of the NLS and Edinburgh University Library. Thomson prints an example of a small amateur collection dated 1870 in 'Heroic Ballad Versions from Glen Urquhart'.

8. Conclusion

The most remarkable aspect of *fianaigheacht* has been its extraordinary adaptability, which has allowed it to remain productive through the entire written history of the Gaelic languages, and to spread into Anglophone literature that has transmitted it across the world. Through translations and adaptations — sometimes transformed into or muddled with Ossian — the Fenian Cycle has influenced literatures and cultures across Europe. This has not been confined to the realm of letters, and this matter has had a broader reach across Europe since the eighteenth century, embracing notable contributions to the visual arts and music as well. This influence places Fionn among a select pantheon whose heroic worlds and lives have been productive and inspirational through centuries, and across cultures: his peers include Homeric and Vergilian heroes, King Arthur, and Charlemagne.

Emerging from a pre-historical obscurity that befits the hero, early references hint at mythological origins or affinities for Fionn and his comrades. In Old Irish literature, a learned elite's interpretation focused on *dinnsheanchas*, and genealogy dominates the texts, yet occasional forays into prose narrative or lyric verse demonstrate the presence of a fully formed tradition, of which only a taste remains extant. By the twelfth century, the parallel development of the framing device of the 'ancients' Oisín and Caoilte, whose personae became the moderators of much of the tradition, along with the growth of heroic narrative verse as a medium of expression, transformed the literature. In post-Norman Ireland, the romance, a form with widespread European currency, came to serve as a less-formal medium for extended narratives. The productivity of the lay and romance continued through at least seven centuries, alongside and interacting with oral tradition, and thousands of texts in these genres survive. The decline of literacy and of the patronage of a Gaelic aristocracy, followed by the decline in the Gaelic languages themselves, resulted in a progressive decrease in new composition from the seventeenth century through to the nineteenth. Nevertheless antiquarianism, and the popularity of — and controversies surrounding — Ossian, led to scholarly investigation of Gaelic literatures, resulting in the publication of authentic texts and their translation into world languages such as English, French, and German. The number of volumes of popular translations, adaptations, and retellings of the medieval and Early Modern tales, aimed at both children and adults, is beyond count; several popular novels re-imagining Fionn have also been written in recent years.

By the opening of the twentieth century, further expansion into other languages and literary cultures occurred, most especially in English, which has brought *fianaigheacht* to a global audience. Some of the first rank of Anglo-Irish authors have embraced the characters of the Fionn Cycle. The young W.B. Yeats assumed Oisín's voice at length in *The Wanderings of Oisin*. James Joyce invokes the character of Fionn, presented according to Heinrich Zimmer's theory as a fusion of Gael and Viking,[1] as a symbol of Dublin.[2] Flann O'Brien's novel *At Swim-Two-Birds* draws deeply on the tradition, importing Fionn and many other characters from traditional and non-traditional literature into a new context. Literary re-appropriation and re-interpretation continue to the present; but their investigation lies outside the parameters of this study of Irish and Scots-Gaelic literature. The literary descendants of Macpherson's Ossian also form an extensive corpus in their own right, whose connections with *fianaigheacht* range from the tenuous to the extensive.

Within the national traditions of Ireland and Scotland in the modern period, however, Fionn has been taken more as an icon than as an active literary character for new composition. As a symbol of the Irish nation, he takes pride of place among the traditional champions and heroes. The nineteenth-century nationalist revival identified with him and his warrior band in such a way that they gave name to its militant movement, the Fenian Brotherhood. In Scotland, Fionn is invoked as the model of the Gael. In both modern languages, the usual phrase for fair play is *co(mh)throm na Féinne*, literally 'the Fenians' equity'.

In the Gaelic languages, despite the continued relevance of Fionn to traditional literature, the active composition of literary *fianaigheacht* has not revived to the extent that it has blossomed in English; it is largely confined either to reworkings of traditional tales or, occasionally, to poetry. Despite the reluctance of recent authors to engage in full-scale *fianaigheacht*, however, allusions are countless and demonstrate the extent to which the older literature serves as a backdrop to the modern. In Irish, such works as the Modern Irish retellings of the main plots within the cycle by Cormac Ó Cadhlaigh in *An Fhiannuidheacht* and Pádraig de Barra's prosimetrum adaptation *Agallamh na Seanóirí* have kept

---

[1] See above p. 66.

[2] MacKillop, *Fionn mac Cumhaill: Celtic Myth in English Literature* has provided an overview of the post-Ossianic and Celtic Revival literature in English with particular focus on James Joyce's use of the character of Fionn.

the traditional literature in accessible circulation — not unlike the writers of the later medieval romances who adapted old plots to the language and tastes of their day. For the same reason, one cannot exclude the efforts of scholars who have published close translations of the older literature in Modern Irish as making a contribution to the vitality of the literary tradition.[3] A few poets, such as Máire Mhac an tSaoi, who has regularly composed in the personae of traditional characters, Fenian and otherwise, have been more creative in their treatment of the cycle than the prose writers; she has written the poems 'Gráinne' and 'Suantraí Ghráinne' in which she explores the emotions associated with Gráinne's elopement using that voice.[4] Between these approaches stands the scholar-poet Pádraig Ó Fiannachta's 26-book poem, *Fianna Éireann*, adapting the plots of numerous tales and lays into an integrated Fenian epic. In Scots Gaelic, where the older literature remains in oral circulation with great veneration for its antiquity (alongside a long memory of the Ossianic forgery), there is greater reluctance to engage in novel composition.

The largest areas of activity in both languages are at liminal points. The parallel oral literature continues, and from it have emerged recordings and published transcriptions of folktales. To fully appreciate these, one must be keenly aware of the required mastery of the traditional story's contents and of the *seanchaidh*'s language and performance skills. This well has not run dry in the international *Gaedhealtacht*. By far the most extensive *fianaigheacht* publications are a special subdivision of this tradition: children's literature. A browse in any bookshop with even a small shelf of Irish or Scots-Gaelic books will generally yield a broader selection for children than for adults. Of these, a large proportion comprises adaptations of traditional stories from literature and folktale, written to inculturate the child with literary heritage while transmitting literacy in the Irish and Scots-Gaelic languages. Fionn and his *fian* will attend many a child's bedside tonight.

Even within the bounds of this investigation, the literature is nearly inexhaustible from the human perspective: more than a century ago, Alfred Nutt estimated that '[w]ere all Ossianic texts preserved in MSS. older than the present [i.e. nineteenth] century to be printed they would fill some eight to ten thousand 8vo pages'.[5] Not only have some additional materials of this nature come to

---

[3] For a discussion of the special value of intra-lingual translation in Irish, see Ó Síocháin, 'Translating *Find and the Phantoms* into Modern Irish'.

[4] In *Margadh na Saoire*.

[5] Nutt, *Ossian and the Ossianic Literature*, 2nd ed., 8.

light in the twentieth century to add to Nutt's count, but it must be recognised that he also excluded the medieval and Early Modern Fenian texts preserved in nineteenth-century manuscripts. No scholar since Nutt has been brave (or foolish) enough to venture a statement in print about the size of the literary corpus. When the whole array is included — with the addition of folklore, modern creative literature and other media — the full Fenian corpus extends beyond the capacity of any one person to read and understand fully. Oisín boasts:

> Da mbeith sgribhionn ₇ peann
> agam dhuit a mhic legheinn
> ní áireomhainn leat no trian
> ar marbh Osgar a ccath ríamh

> Had I script and pen for you, O student, I could not reckon the half or the third of all whom Osgur ever killed in battle.[6]

He made no idle boast, especially when others still continue to take up the task of writing on his behalf.

---

[6] *DF* ii, 286–7, §138.

Bibliography

Almqvist, B., S. Ó Catháin and P. Ó Héalaí (eds), *The Heroic Process: Form, Function, and Fantasy in Folk Epic* (Dublin, 1987). The Fenian papers in this work were also published in *Béaloideas* 54–5 (1986–7) with the same pagination. Some copies of the *Béaloideas* volume were later distributed with different covers under the title *Fiannaíocht: Essays on the Fenian Tradition of Ireland and Scotland* (Dublin, 1987).

Anonymous [C.H. Wilson], *Select Irish Poems Translated into English* (no publication information provided, *c*. 1792).

Anonymous [L.C. Stern], Review of K. Meyer, L.C. Stern, R. Thurneysen, F. Sommer, W. Foy, A. Leskien, K. Brugmann and E. Windisch (eds), *Festschrift Whitley Stokes*, in 'Erschienene Schriften', *Zeitschrift für celtische Philologie* 3 (1901) 432–4.

Anonymous [probably K. Meyer], Review of K. Meyer, *Fianaigecht*, in 'Erschienene Schriften', *Zeitschrift für celtische Philologie* 8 (1912) 599.

Arbuthnot, S., 'Finn, Ferchess, and the *Rincne*: Versions Compared', in Arbuthnot and Parsons (eds), *The Gaelic Finn Tradition*, 62–80.

— 'On the Name Oscar and Two Little-known Episodes Involving the *Fían*', *Cambrian Medieval Celtic Studies* 51 (Summer 2006) 67–81.

— 'Some Accretions to Genealogical Material in a Manuscript Boxed with the Book of Leinster', *Zeitschrift für celtische Philologie* 55 (2006) 57–67.

— and G. Parsons (eds), *The Gaelic Finn Tradition* (Dublin, 2012).

Baumgarten, R., 'Etymological Aetiology in Irish Tradition', *Ériu* 41 (1990) 115–22.

— 'Placenames, Etymology, and the Structure of *Fianaigecht*', in Almqvist, Ó Catháin and Ó Héalaí (eds), *The Heroic Process*, 1–24.

Bergin, O. and J. MacNeill (Gaelicised in reprints as O. Ó hAimhirgin and E. Mac Néill), *Eachtra Lomnochtáin: Irish Text*, Gaelic League Publications (Dublin, 1901; reprints 1903, 1905). Originally serialised in *The Gaelic Journal / Irisleabhar na Gaedhilge* 8–9 (1897–9) as *Eachtra Lomnochtáin an tSléibhe Riffe* (with an English translation).

Best, R.I. and O. Bergin, *Lebor na hUidre: The Book of the Dun Cow* (Dublin, 1929).

—, O. Bergin, M.A. O'Brien and A. O'Sullivan, *The Book of Leinster, Formerly Lebor na Núachongbála*, 6 vols (Dublin, 1954–83).

Binchy, D. 'The Passing of the Old Order', in Ó Cuív (ed.), *The Impact of the Scandinavian Invasions on the Celtic-speaking Peoples*, 119–32.

Black, G.F., *Macpherson's Ossian and the Ossianic Controversy: A Contribution Towards a Bibliography* (New York, 1926).

Breatnach, C., 'Cath Fionntrágha', in Ó Fiannachta (ed.), *An Fhiannaíocht*, 128–43.

— 'Early Modern Irish Prose', in K. McCone and K. Simms (eds), *Progress in Medieval Irish Studies* (Maynooth, 1996) 189–206.

— 'The Historical Context of *Cath Fionntrágha*', *Éigse* 28 (1995) 138–55.

— 'The Transmission and Text of *Tóruigheacht Dhiarmada agus Ghráinne*:

A Re-appraisal', in Arbuthnot and Parsons (eds), *The Gaelic Finn Tradition*, 139–50.

Breatnach, R.A., 'The End of a Tradition: A Survey of Eighteenth-century Gaelic Literature', *Studia Hibernica* 1 (1961) 128–50.

Broderick, G., 'Fin as Oshin', *Celtica* 21 (1990) 51–60.

Brooke, C., *Reliques of Irish Poetry: Consisting of Heroic Poems, Odes, Elegies, and Songs, Translated into English Verse* (Dublin, 1789; reprints Perth, 1816; Dublin, 2009 with an introduction, new literal translations, and commentaries by L. Ní Mhunghaile).

Bruford, A., *Gaelic Folk-tales and Mediaeval Romances* (published as *Béaloideas* 34 [1966]).

— 'Oral and Literary Fenian Tales', in Almqvist, Ó Catháin and Ó Héalaí (eds), *The Heroic Process*, 25–56.

Cameron, A., 'Poems of Ossian Collected by John McDonald in the Western Parishes of Strathnaver, Ross, and Inverness-shire, in September and October, 1805', *Transactions of the Gaelic Society of Inverness* 13 (1888) 269–300.

— *Reliquiae Celticae: Texts, Papers and Studies in Gaelic Literature and Philosophy Left by the late Rev. Alexander Cameron, Ll.D.*, eds A. McBain and J. Kennedy, 2 vols (Inverness, 1892–4).

Campbell, J.F., *Leabhar na Feinne: Vol. 1. Gaelic Texts. Heroic Gaelic Ballads collected in Scotland chiefly from 1512 to 1871* (London, 1872; reprint Shannon, 1972).

— *Popular Tales of the West Highlands*, 4 vols (Edinburgh, 1862; reprint [different pagination] Paisley, 1890).

Campbell, J.G. (introduction by A. Nutt), *The Fians: or, Stories, Poems, & Traditions of Fionn and his Warrior Band*, Waifs and Strays of Celtic Tradition, Argyllshire Series 4 (London, 1891).

Carey, J., '*Acallam na Senórach*: A Conversation between Worlds', in Arbuthnot and Parsons (eds), *The Gaelic Finn Tradition*, 76–89.

— (ed.), *Duanaire Finn: Reassessments*, Irish Texts Society Subsidiary Series 13 (London, 2003).

— 'Nōdons, Lugus, Windos', in C.M. Ternes and H. Zinser (eds), *Dieux des Celtes / Goetter der Kelten / Gods of the Celts* (Luxembourg, 2002) 99–126.

— 'Remarks on Dating', in idem (ed.), *Duanaire Finn: Reassessments*, 1–18.

— 'Two Notes on Names', *Éigse* 35 (2005) 116–24.

Carney, J., 'Language and Literature to 1169', in D. Ó Cróinín (ed.), *A New History of Ireland. I: Prehistoric and Early Ireland* (Oxford, 2005) 451–510.

— 'Literature in Irish', in A. Cosgrove (ed.), *A New History of Ireland. II: Medieval Ireland 1169–1534* (Oxford, 1987) 688–707.

— 'Three Old-Irish Accentual Poems', *Ériu* 22 (1971) 23–80.

— 'Two Poems from Acallam na Senórach', in J. Carney and D. Greene (eds), *Celtic Studies: Essays in Memory of Angus Matheson* (London, 1968) 22–32.

Céitinn, S. [G. Keating], *Foras Feasa ar Éirinn*, ed. and trans. D. Comyn [vol. 1] and P. Dinneen [vols 2–4], 4 vols, Irish Texts Society 4, 8, 9, 15 (London 1902–14).

Chadbourne, K., 'The Voices of Hounds: Heroic Dogs and Men in the Finn Ballads and Tales', in J.F. Nagy and L. Jones (eds), *Heroic Poets and Poetic Heroes in Celtic Tradition: A Festschrift for Patrick K. Ford*, CSANA Yearbook 3–4 (Dublin, 2005) 28–41.

Christiansen, R.Th., *The Vikings and Viking Wars in Irish and Gaelic Tradition*, Skrifter Utgitt av Det Norske Videnskaps-Akademi i Oslo II. Hist.-Filos. Klasse 1930. No. 1 (Oslo, 1931).

Clover, C., 'The Long Prose Form', *Arkiv för Nordisk Filologi* 101 (1986) 10–39.

Colgan, J. (ed.), [*Acta Sanctorum Hiberniae*] *Acta Sanctorum Veteris et Maioris Scotiae seu Hiberniae Sanctorum Insulae* (Lovanii, 1645; reprint Dublin, 1947).

— (ed.), [*Trias Thaumaturga*] *Triadis Thaumaturgae seu Divorum Patricii Columbae et Brigidae, Trium Veteris et Maioris Scotiae seu Hiberniae Sanctorum Insulae* (Lovanii, 1647; reprint Dublin, 1997).

Connellan, O., 'On the Fians of Erin and the Poems of Oisin, the Celebrated Bard', in idem (ed.), *Transactions of the Ossianic Society, for the Year 1857. Vol. V. Imtheacht na Tromdhaimhe* (Dublin, 1860) 204–27.

— 'The Poems of Ossian by Macpherson', in idem (ed.), *Transactions of the Ossianic Society, for the Year 1857. Vol. V. Imtheacht na Tromdhaimhe* (Dublin, 1860) 171–204.

Connon, A., 'Plotting *Acallam na Senórach*: The Physical Context of the "Mayo" Sequence', in S. Sheehan, J. Findon and W. Follett (eds), *Gablánach in Scélaigecht: Celtic Studies in Honour of Ann Dooley* (Dublin, 2013) 69–102.

— 'The Roscommon *Locus* of *Acallam na Senórach* and Some Thoughts as to *Tempus* and *Persona*', in Doyle and Murray (eds), *In Dialogue with the Agallamh*, 21–59.

Corthals, J., 'The Rhymeless "Leinster poems"', *Celtica* 21 (1990) 111–25.

— 'Die Trennung von Finn und Gráinne', *Zeitschrift für celtische Philologie* 49–50 (1997) 71–91.

Craoibhín, An [pseudonym of D. Hyde], 'An Agallamh Bheag', *Lia Fáil* 1 (1924) 79–107.

Curley, T.M., *Samuel Johnson, the Ossian Fraud, and the Celtic Revival in Great Britain and Ireland* (Cambridge, 2009; reprint 2014).

Curteis, E. [E. Curtis], 'Age and Origin of the Fenian Tales', *Journal of the Ivernian Society* 1 (1908–9) 159–68.

d'Arbois de Jubainville, H., *Cours de la Littérature Celtique*, 12 vols (Paris, 1883–1902).

— Review of H. Zimmer, 'Keltische Beiträge III', *Revue Celtique* 12 (1891) 295–300.

de Barra, P., *Agallamh na Seanóirí*, Saíocht ár Sean 6–7, 2 vols (Baile Átha Cliath 1984–6).

Dillon, M., *Stories from the Acallam*, Mediaeval and Modern Irish Series 23 (Dublin, 1970; reprint 1984).

—, C. Mooney and P. de Brún, *Catalogue of Irish Manuscripts in the Franciscan Library, Killiney* (Dublin, 1969).

Donahue, A., 'The *Acallam na Senórach*: A Medieval Instruction Manual', *Proceedings of the Harvard Celtic Colloquium* 24–5 (2004–5) 206–14.

Dooley, A., 'The Date and Purpose of *Acallam na Senórach*', *Éigse* 34 (2004) 97–126.

— 'The Deployment of Some Hagiographical Sources in *Acallam na Senórach*', in Arbuthnot and Parsons (eds), *The Gaelic Finn Tradition*, 97–110.

— 'The European Context of *Acallam na Senórach*', in Doyle and Murray (eds), *In Dialogue with the Agallamh*, 60–75.

— and H. Roe, *Tales of the Elders of Ireland: A New Translation of Acallam na Senórach* (Oxford, 1999).

Doyle, A. and K. Murray (eds), *In Dialogue with the Agallamh: Essays in Honour of Seán Ó Coileáin* (Dublin, 2014).

Dunn, J.J., 'Macpherson's Ossian and the Ossianic Controversy: A Supplementary Bibliography', *Bulletin of the New York Public Library* 75 (1971) 465–73.

Enright, M.J., 'Fires of Knowledge: A Theory of Warband Education in Medieval Ireland and Homeric Greece', in P. Ní Chatháin and M. Richter (eds), *Ireland and Europe in the Early Middle Ages: Texts and Transmission* (Dublin, 2002) 342–67.

Falileyev, A., in collaboration with A.E. Gohil and N. Ward, *Dictionary of Continental Celtic Place-names: A Celtic Companion to the Barrington Atlas of the Greek and Roman World* (Aberystwyth, 2010).

Fischer, L., 'Fionn mac Cumhaill among the Old English: Some Comments on the Book of Howth' (forthcoming).

Flahive, J.J. '*A Chloidhimh Chléirchín in Chluig* and the Concept of the Literary Cycle in Mediaeval Ireland' (forthcoming).

— 'Caoilte's Sword: Edition and Translation' (forthcoming).

— 'A Hero's Lament: Aithbhreac Inghean Coirceadail's Lament for Niall Óg Mac Néill', *Scottish Studies* 35 (2010) 106–19.

— 'The Relic Lays: A Study in the Development of Late Middle-Gaelic *Fianaigheacht*', unpublished Ph.D. thesis (University of Edinburgh, 2004).

— 'Revisiting the Reeves *Agallamh*', in Doyle and Murray (eds), *In Dialogue with the Agallamh*, 164–84.

— 'The Shield of Fionn: The Poem *Uchán a sciath mo rígh réigh* in Leabhar Ua Maine', in J. Carey, K. Murray and C. Ó Dochartaigh (eds), *Sacred Histories: A Festschrift for Máire Herbert* (Dublin, 2015) 139–60.

Foley, J.M., *Immanent Art: From Structure to Meaning in Traditional Oral Epic* (Bloomington, Indiana, 1991).

Gaskill, H. (ed.), *Ossian Revisited* (Edinburgh, 1991).

— (ed.), *The Poems of Ossian and Related Works: James Macpherson*, with an Introduction by F. Stafford (Edinburgh, 1996).

— (ed.), *The Reception of Ossian in Europe*, The Athlone Critical Traditions Series: The Reception of British Authors in Europe (London and New York, 2004).

Gillies, E. [Eoin, also named as John], *A Collection of Ancient and Modern Gaelic Poems and Songs / Dain agus Orain Ghaidhealach* (Perth, 1786).

Gillies, W., 'Heroes and Ancestors', in Almqvist, Ó Catháin and Ó Héalaí (eds), *The Heroic Process*, 57–74.

— 'An Irish Manuscript in Scotland, *Scottish Gaelic Studies* 13 (1978) 127–9.

Gunderloch, A., 'The *Cath Gabhra* Family of Ballads: A Study in Textual Relationships', unpublished Ph.D. Thesis (University of Edinburgh, 1997).

— 'Duncan Kennedy and His Heroic Ballads', in Arbuthnot and Parsons (eds), *The Gaelic Finn Tradition*, 197–94.

Gwynn, E.J., 'The Burning of Finn's House', *Ériu* 1 (1904) 13–37.

— *The Metrical Dindshenchas*, 5 vols, Todd Lecture Series 8–12 (Dublin, 1903–35; reprint 1991).

Harmon, M., *The Dialogue of the Ancients of Ireland: A New Translation of Acallam na Senórach* (Dublin, 2001; reprint 2009).

Hennessy, W., 'The Battle of Cnucha', *Revue Celtique* 2 (1872–3) 86–93.

Highland Society of London (eds), *The Poems of Ossian, in the Original Gaelic, with a Literal Translation into Latin by the Late Robert Mac-Farlan, A.M.*, 3 vols (London, Edinburgh and Dublin, 1807).

Hill, T.F., *Antient Erse Poems Collected among the Scottish Highlands, in Order to Illustrate the Ossian of Mr Macpherson* (London, 1784); originally published serially as 'New Lights on the Ossian Controversy', in *Gentleman's Magazine*, 52–4 (1782–3).

Hirschfeld, O. and C. Zangmeister (eds), *Corpus Inscriptionum Latinarum XIII: Inscriptiones Trium Galliarum et Germanorum Latinae* (Berolini, 1905).

Hollo, K., '"Finn and the Man in the Tree" as Verbal Icon', in Arbuthnot and Parsons (eds), *The Gaelic Finn Tradition*, 50–61.

Hull, V., 'A Rhetoric in *Finn and the Man in the Tree*', *Zeitschrift für celtische Philologie* 30 (1967) 17–20.

— 'Two Tales about Find', *Speculum* 16 (1941) 322–33.

Hyde, D., 'The Reeves Manuscript of "Agallamh na Seanórach"', *Revue Celtique* 38 (1921) 289–95.

— and T. Ó Caomhánaigh (eds), 'Cuireadh Mhaoil Uí Mhananáin ar Fionn mac Cumhaill agus Fianaibh Éirionn', *Lia Fail* 3 (1930) 87–114.

Innes, S., 'Fionn and Ailbhe's Riddles between Ireland and Scotland', in M. Boyd (ed.), *Ollam: Studies in Gaelic and Related Traditions in Honor of Tomás Ó Cathasaigh* (Madison and Teaneck, 2016) 271–85.

Jackson, K., *Studies in Early Celtic Nature Poetry* (Cambridge, 1935).

Jerram, C.S., *Dàn an Deirg, agus Tiomna Ghuill (Dargo and Gaul): Two Poems from Dr Smith's Collection Entitled Sean Dàna* (Edinburgh and London, 1874).

— 'Some Causes of the Imperfect Appreciation by Englishmen of the Ossianic Poems', *Transactions of the Gaelic Society of Inverness* 5 (1875–6) 97–110.

Joyce, P.W., *Old Celtic Romances* (London, 1879; reprint Dublin, 1961).

Joynt, M., *Feis Tighe Chonáin*, Mediaeval and Modern Irish Series 7 (Dublin, 1936).

Kinsella, T., *The Táin: Translated from the Irish Epic Táin Bó Cuailnge* (Oxford, 1970; reprints Dublin, 1985; Oxford, 2002).

Koch, J. and J. Carey, *The Celtic Heroic Age* (2nd ed., Andover, Massachusetts, 1997).

Krause, D., 'The Hidden Oisín', *Studia Hibernica* 6 (1966) 7–24.

Kühns, J.S., 'An Edition and Translation of the *Agallamh Bheag* in the Book of Lismore', unpublished M.Phil. thesis (University of Glasgow, 2006).

— 'Some Observations on the *Acallam Bec*', in Arbuthnot and Parsons (eds), *The Gaelic Finn Tradition*, 122–38.

Laoide, S., *Fian-laoithe* (Baile Átha Cliath, 1917).

Mac Airt, S. and G. Mac Niocaill, *The Annals of Ulster (to A.D. 1131)* (Dublin, 1983).

Mhac an tSaoi, M., *Margadh na Saoire* (Baile Átha Cliath, 1956).

M'Callum, H. and J. M'Callum, *An Original Collection of the Poems of Ossian, Orran, Ulin, and Other Bards Who Flourished in the Same Age*, 2 vols (Montrose, 1816).

Mac Cana, P., '*Fianaigecht* in the Pre-Norman Period', in Almqvist, Ó Catháin and Ó Héalaí (eds), *The Heroic Process*, 75–99.

— 'The Influence of the Vikings on Celtic Literature', in Ó Cuív (ed.), *The Impact of the Scandinavian Invasions on the Celtic-speaking Peoples*, 78–118.

— *The Learned Tales of Medieval Ireland* (Dublin, 1980).

McCone, K., 'The Celtic and Indo-European Origins of the *Fian*', in Arbuthnot and Parsons (eds), *The Gaelic Finn Tradition*, 14–30.

— 'Cúlra Ind-Eorpach na Féinne', in Ó Fiannachta (ed.), *An Fhiannaíocht*, 7–29.

— 'Hund, Wolf und Krieger bei den Indogermanen', in W. Meid (ed.), *Studien zum indogermanischen Wortschatz* (Innsbruck, 1987) 101–54.

— 'Werewolves, Cyclopes, *Díberga* and *Fíanna*: Juvenile Delinquency in Early Ireland', *Cambridge Medieval Celtic Studies* 12 (Winter 1986) 1–22.

Mac Craith, M., 'Charles Wilson (*c*. 1756–1808): Réamhtheachtaí Charlotte Brooke', *Eighteenth-century Ireland. Iris an Dá Chultúr* 17 (2002) 57–78.

— 'The "Forging" of Ossian', in T. Brown (ed.), *Celticism*, Studia Imagologica: Amsterdam Studies on Cultural Identity 8 (Amsterdam and Atlanta, 1996) 125–41.

— 'Tadhg Ó Cianáin: Spaghetti *Fiannaigheacht*', in Arbuthnot and Parsons (eds), *The Gaelic Finn Tradition*, 163–78.

— '"We Know All These Poems": The Irish Response to *Ossian*', in Gaskill (ed.), *The Reception of Ossian in Europe*, 91–108.

MacDougall, J. (introduction by A. Nutt), *Folk and Hero Tales*, Waifs and Strays of Celtic Tradition, Argyllshire Series 3 (London, 1891).

MacInnes, J., *Folk and Hero Tales* (including 'Development of the Fenian or

Ossianic Saga' by A. Nutt), Waifs and Strays of Celtic Tradition, Argyllshire Series 2 (London, 1890).

Mackenzie, H., *Report of the Highland Society of Scotland, Appointed to Enquire into the Nature and Authenticity of the Poems of Ossian* (Edinburgh, 1805).

MacKillop, J., *Fionn Mac Cumhaill: Celtic Myth in English Literature* (Syracuse, 1986).

MacKinnon, D., 'Collection of Ossianic Ballads by Jerome Stone', *Transactions of the Gaelic Society of Inverness* 14 (1889) 314–69.

M'Lauchlan, T., *The Dean of Lismore's Book: A Selection of Ancient Gaelic Poetry from a Manuscript Made by Sir James M'Gregor, Dean of Lismore, in the Beginning of the Sixteenth Century ... and an Introduction and Additional Notes by William F. Skene Esq.* (Edinburgh, 1862).

MacLean, M., *The Literature of the Celts* (London and Glasgow, 1926).

MacNeill, E. [vol. 1] and G. Murphy [vols 2 and 3], *Duanaire Finn: The Book of the Lays of Finn*, 3 vols, Irish Texts Society 4, 33, 54 (London, 1904–53).

Mac Piarais, P., *Bruidhean Chaorthainn* (Baile Átha Cliath, 1908).

McQuillan, P., 'Finn, Fothad, and *Fian*: Some Early Associations', *Proceedings of the Harvard Celtic Colloquium* 8 (1988) 1–10.

Meek, D.E., 'The Banners of the Fian in Gaelic Ballad Tradition', *Cambridge Medieval Celtic Studies* 11 (Summer 1986) 29–69.

— 'The Corpus of Heroic Verse in the Book of the Dean of Lismore', 2 vols, unpublished Ph.D. thesis (University of Glasgow, 1982).

— 'The Death of Diarmaid in Scottish and Irish Tradition', *Celtica* 21 (1990) 335–61.

— 'Development and Degeneration in Gaelic Ballad Texts', in Almqvist, Ó Catháin and Ó Héalaí (eds), *The Heroic Process*, 131–60.

— '*Duanaire Finn* and Gaelic Scotland', in Carey (ed.), *Duanaire Finn: Reassessments*, 19–38.

— 'The Gaelic Ballads of Scotland: Creativity and Adaptation', in Gaskill (ed.), *Ossian Revisited*, 19–48.

— '"Norsemen and Noble Stewards": The MacSween Poem in the Book of the Dean of Lismore', *Cambrian Medieval Celtic Studies* 34 (Winter, 1997) 1–49.

— 'Place-names and Literature: Evidence from the Gaelic Ballads', in S. Taylor (ed.), *The Uses of Place-names* (Edinburgh, 1998) 147–68.

— 'The Scots-Gaelic Scribes of Late Medieval Perthshire: An Overview of the Orthography and Contents of the Book of the Dean of Lismore', in J.D. McClure and M. Spiller (eds), *Bryght Lanterns: Essays on the Language and Literature of Medieval and Renaissance Scotland* (Aberdeen, 1989) 387–404.

Meyer, K., 'The Boyish Exploits of Finn', *Ériu* 1 (1904) 180–90.

— 'Cáilte Cecinit. Book of Leinster, p. 208a', *Ériu* 1 (1903) 72–3.

— *Cath Finntrága or Battle of Ventry Edited from MS. Rawl. B. 487*, in the Bodleian Library, Anecdota Oxoniensia Mediaeval and Modern Series, vol. 1 part 4 (Oxford, 1885).

— *Fianaigecht: Being a Collection of Hitherto Inedited Irish Poems and Tales Relating to Finn and his Fiana*, Todd Lecture Series 16 (Dublin, 1910; reprints 1937, 1993).
— 'Find and the Man in the Tree', *Revue Celtique* 25 (1904) 344–9.
— 'Finn and Grainne', *Zeitschrift für celtische Philologie* 1 (1897) 458–61.
— *Four Old-Irish Songs of Summer and Winter* (London, 1903).
— *The Instructions of King Cormac Mac Airt*, Todd Lecture Series 15 (Dublin, 1909).
— 'Macgnímartha Find', *Revue Celtique* 5 (1881–3) 195–204.
— Review of H. Zimmer, 'Keltische Beiträge I', *Revue Celtique* 10 (1889) 360–9.
— 'Two Tales about Finn', *Revue Celtique* 14 (1893) 241–9.
Moore, D., *Ossian and Ossianism*, 4 vols (London, 2003).
Murphy, G., *Early Irish Lyrics* (Oxford, 1956; reprints 1998, 2007).
— *The Ossianic Lore and Romantic Tales of Medieval Ireland*, Irish Life and Culture 11 (Dublin, 1955; reprint Cork, 1961; revised ed. by B. Ó Cuív, Dublin, 1971).
— *Saga and Myth in Ancient Ireland*, Irish Life and Culture 10 (Dublin, 1955; reprint Cork, 1961).
Murray, K., 'Interpreting the Evidence: Problems with Dating the Early *Fianaigecht* Corpus', in Arbuthnot and Parsons (eds), *The Gaelic Finn Tradition*, 31–49.
— 'The Reworking of Old Irish Narrative Texts in the Middle Irish Period: Contexts and Motivations', in E. Boyle and D. Hayden (eds), *Authorities and Adaptations: The Reworking and Transmission of Textual Sources in the Middle Ages* (Dublin, 2015) 293–308.
— 'The Treatment of Place-names in the Early Fíanaigecht Corpus', in E. Purcell, P. MacCotter, J. Nyhan and J. Sheehan (eds), *Clerics, Kings and Vikings: Essays on Medieval Ireland in Honour of Donnchadh Ó Corráin* (Dublin, 2015) 452–7.
Nagy, J.F., '*Acallam na Senórach*: A Tri-cycle', in D.M. Wiley (ed.), *Essays on the Early Irish King Tales* (Dublin, 2008) 68–83.
— 'Compositional Concerns in the *Acallam na Senórach*', in Ó Corráin, Breatnach and McCone (eds), *Sages, Saints and Storytellers*, 149–58.
— 'Heroic Destinies in the *Macgnímrada* of Finn and Cú Chulainn', *Zeitschrift für celtische Philologie* 40 (1984) 25–39.
— 'In Defence of Rómánsaíocht', *Ériu* 38 (1987) 9–26.
— 'Keeping the *Acallam* Together', in Arbuthnot and Parsons (eds), *The Gaelic Finn Tradition*, 111–21.
— 'Life in the Fast Lane: The *Acallam na Senórach*', in H. Fulton (ed.), *Medieval Celtic Literature and Society* (Dublin, 2005) 117–31.
— 'Observations on the Ossianesque', *Journal of American Folklore* 114 (2001) 436–46.
— 'Oral Tradition in the *Acallam na Senórach*', in W.H.F. Nicolaison (ed.), *Oral Traditions in the Middle Ages*, Medieval and Renaissance Texts and Studies 112 (Binghamton, New York, 1995) 77–95.
— 'Some Strands and Strains in *Acallam na Senórach*', in Doyle and Murray

(eds), *In Dialogue with the Agallamh*, 90–108.

— *The Wisdom of the Outlaw: The Boyhood Deeds of Finn in Gaelic Narrataive Tradition* (London, Berkeley and Los Angeles, 1985).

Ní Mhaonaigh, M., 'Pagans and Holy Men: Literary Manifestations of Twelfth-century Reform', in D. Bracken and D. Ó Riain-Raedel (eds), *Ireland and Europe in the Twelfth Century: Reform and Renewal* (Dublin, 2006) 143–61.

Ní Mhuirgheasa, M., *Imtheacht an Dá Nónbhar agus Tóraigheacht Taise Taoibhghile*, Leabhair ó Láimhsgríbhnibh 16 [*bis, recte* 17] (Baile Átha Cliath, 1954).

— and S. Ó Ceithearnaigh, *Sgéalta Rómánsuíochta*, Leabhair ó Láimhsgríbhnibh 16 (Baile Átha Cliath, 1952).

Ní Mhurchú, S., '*Agallamh Oisín agus Phádraig*: Composition and Transmission', in Arbuthnot and Parsons (eds), *The Gaelic Finn Tradition*, 195–208.

— *Agallamh Oisín agus Phádraig*: The Growth of an Ossianic Lay', in S. Zimmer (ed.), *Kelten am Rhein: Akten des dreizehnten Internationalen Kelologiekongresses / Proceedings of the Thirteenth International Congress of Celtic Studies, 23. Bis 27. Juli 2007 in Bonn. Zweiter Teil. Philologie, Sprachen und Literaturen*, Beihefte der Bonner Jahrbücher 58 (Mainz am Rhein, 2009) 175–80.

— 'An tAgallamh Nua: Athleagan Déanach d'Agallamh na Seanórach', in Doyle and Murray (eds), *In Dialogue with the Agallamh*, 185–216.

Ní Shéaghdha, N., *Agallamh na Senórach*, 3 vols, Leabhair ó Láimhsgríbhnibh 7, 10, 15 (Baile Átha Cliath, 1942–5; reprint in one vol., London, 2014).

— 'Bruighion Bheag na hAlmhan', in Ní Shéaghdha and Ní Mhuirgheasa, *Trí Bruidhne*, 16–39.

— *Tóraigheacht Dhiarmada agus Ghráinne* (Baile Átha Cliath, 1944; reprint 1962).

— *Tóruigheacht Dhiarmada agus Ghráinne*, Irish Texts Society 48 (Dublin, 1967).

— and M. Ní Mhuirgheasa, *Trí Bruidhne*, Leabhair ó Láimhsgríbhnibh 2 (Baile Átha Cliath, 1941).

Nuner, R.D., 'The Verbal System of the *Agallamh na Senórach*', *Zeitschrift für celtische Philologie* 27 (1958–9) 230–310.

Nutt, A., 'Celtic Myth and Saga — A Survey of Recent Literature', *The Archaeological Review* 2 (1888) 110–42.

— 'A New Theory of the Ossianic Saga', *Academy and Literature* 39 (1891) 161–3, 235.

— *Ossian and the Ossianic Literature*, Popular Studies in Mythology, Romance and Folklore 3 (London, 1899; 2nd rev. ed., London, 1910).

Ó Baoighill, P. and M. (eds), *Amhráin Hiúdaí Fheilimí agus Laoithe Fiannaíochta as Rann na Feirste* ('Preas Uladh'; no publication information provided).

Ó Béarra, F., 'A Critical Edition of Siaburcharpat Con Culaind', unpublished Ph.D. thesis (National University of Ireland, Galway, 2004).

— *Síaburcharpat Con Culainn: A Critical Edition with Introduction, Notes, Bibliography and Glossary*, Maynooth Medieval Irish Texts (Maynooth, forthcoming).

O'Beirne Crowe, J., 'Siabur-charbat Con Culaind. From "Leabor na h-Uidre" (fol. 37 et seqq.), a Manuscript of the Royal Irish Academy', *Journal of the Royal Historical and Archaeological Society of Ireland*, Ser. 4, vol. 1 (1870) 384–91.

Ó Briain, M., 'The Conception and Birth of Fionn mac Cumhaill's Canine Cousin', in A. Ahlqvist, G.W. Banks, R. Latvio, H. Nyberg and T. Sjöblom (eds), *Celtica Helsingiensia: Proceedings from a Symposium on Celtic Studies*, Societas Scientarum Fennica, Commentationes Humanarum Litterarum 107 (Helsinki, 1996) 179–202.

— '*Duanaire Finn* XXII: Goll and the Champion's Portion', in Carey (ed.), *Duanaire Finn: Reassessments*, 51–78.

— '*Laoidh Cholainn gan Chionn*', in R. Black, W. Gillies and R. Ó Maolalaigh (eds), *Celtic Connections: Proceedings of the 10th International Congress of Celtic Studies*, vol. 1 (East Linton, 1999) 233–50.

— 'Oisín's Biography: Conception and Birth', in H.L.C. Tristram (ed.), *Text and Zeittiefe*, ScriptOralia 58 (Tübingen, 1994) 455–86.

— 'Some Material on Oisín in the Land of Youth', in Ó Corráin, Breatnach and McCone (eds), *Sages, Saints and Storytellers*, 181–99.

— 'Suirghe Fhinn', in Ó Fiannachta (ed.), *An Fhiannaíocht*, 69–95.

O'Brien, F., *At Swim-Two-Birds* (London, 1939 and multiple reprints).

Ó Cadhla, S., 'Gods and Heroes: Approaching the *Acallam* as Ethnography', in Doyle and Murray (eds), *In Dialogue with the Agallamh*, 125–43.

Ó Cadhlaigh, C., *An Fhiannuidheacht* (Baile Átha Cliath, 1938).

Ó Canainn, P. (ed.), *Diarmuid ⁊ Gráinne / An Giolla Deacair / Bodach an Chóta Lachtna* (Baile Átha Cliath, 1939).

Ó Catháin, D., 'General Baron Edmond Harold (1737–1808): A Celtic Writer in Germany', *Studia Hibernica* 30 (1998–9) 119–53.

Ó Cathasaigh, T., '*Cath Maige Tuired* as Exemplary Myth', in P. de Brún, S. Ó Coileáin and P. Ó Riain (eds), *Folia Gadelica: Aistí ó Iardhaltaí leis a Bronnadh ar R.A. Breatnach, M.A., M.R.I.A.* (Cork, 1983) 1–19.

— 'Tóraíocht Dhiarmada agus Ghráinne', in Ó Fiannachta (ed.), *An Fhiannaíocht*, 30–46.

Ó Coileáin, S., 'Place and Placename in *Fianaigheacht*', *Studia Hibernica* 27 (1993) 45–60; reprinted in Doyle and Murray (eds), *In Dialogue with the Agallamh*, 6–20.

— 'The Setting of *Géisid Cúan*', in J. Carey, M. Herbert and K. Murray (eds), *Cín Chille Cúile: Texts, Saints and Places. Essays in Honour of Pádraig Ó Riain* (Aberystwth, 2004) 234–48; reprinted in Doyle and Murray (eds), *In Dialogue with the Agallamh*, 218–30.

O'Connell, J., '*Airem Muinntari Finn* and *Anmonna Oesa Fedma Find*: Manuscripts, Scribes, and Texts', unpublished M.A. thesis (University College Cork, 2012).

O'Conor, C., *A Dissertation on the First Migrations, and Final Settlement of the Scots in the North-Britain; With Occasional Observations on the*

Poems of Fingal and Temora (Dublin, 1766).

— *Dissertations on the Antient History of Ireland: Wherein an Account is given of the Origine, Government, Letters, Sciences, Religion, Manners and Customs, of the Antient Inhabitants* (Dublin, 1753).

Ó Corráin, D., L. Breatnach and K. McCone (eds), *Sages, Saints and Storytellers: Studies in Honour of Professor James Carney*, Maynooth Monographs 2 (Maynooth, 1989).

Ó Cróinín, B., 'Bruíonta na Féinne', in S. Ó Coileáin, L. Ó Múrchú and P. Riggs (eds), *Séimhfhear Suairc: Aistí in Ómós don Ollamh Breandán Ó Conchúir* (An Daingean, 2013) 480–501.

Ó Cuív, B., (ed.), *The Impact of the Scandinavian Invasions on the Celtic-speaking Peoples c. 800–1100 A.D.: Introductory Papers Read at Plenary Sessions of the International Congress of Celtic Studies, held in Dublin, 6–10 July, 1959* (Baile Átha Cliath, 1975).

— 'Miscellanea 2: Agallamh Fhinn agus Ailbhe', *Celtica* 18 (1986) 111–15.

O'Curry, E., *Lectures on the Manuscript Materials of Ancient Irish History* (Dublin, 1861, reprints Dublin 1872, 1873, 1878, 1995; London, 1873).

O'Daly, J., 'Laoithe Fiannuigheachta; or, Fenian Poems', in idem (ed.), *Transactions of the Ossianic Society, for the Year 1856. Vol. IV. Laoithe Fianuigheachta* (Dublin, 1859) 1–280.

— 'Laoithe Fiannuigheachta; or, Fenian Poems, Second Series', in idem (ed.), *Transactions of the Ossianic Society, for the Year 1858. Vol. VI. Laoithe Fianuigheachta* (Dublin, 1861) 1–207.

O Daly, M., *Cath Maige Mucrama*, Irish Texts Society 50 (London, 1975).

Ó Donnchadha, T., .i. Torna, *Óir-chiste Fiannuíochta* (Baile Átha Cliath, [no date]).

O'Donovan, J., [*Annals of the Four Masters*] *Annála Ríoghachta Éireann: Annals of the Kingdom of Ireland, by the Four Masters, from the Earliest Times to the Year 1616*, 7 vols (Dublin, 1848–51; reprints 1856, 1990).

— 'Mac-gnimartha Finn Mac Cumaill', in J. O'Daly (ed.), *Transactions of the Ossianic Society for the Year 1856. Vol. IV. Laoithe Fiannuigheachta* (1859) 281–304.

Ó Dubhthaigh, B., 'Agallamh Oisín agus Phádraig: "Lá dhúinne ar Sliabh Fuaid"', *Éigse* 9 (1958) 34–42.

Ó Fiannachta, P., 'The Development of the Debate between Pádraig and Oisín', in Almqvist, Ó Catháin and Ó Héalaí (eds), *The Heroic Process*, 183–206.

— (ed.), *An Fhiannaíocht*, Léachtaí Cholm Cille 25 (Maigh Nuad, 1995).

— *Fianna Éireann: Eipic ar an bhFiannaíocht idir Laoithe agus Scéalta* (An Daingean, 2014).

Ó Flannghaile, T., *Laoi Oisín ar Thír na n-Óg: The Lay of Oisín in the Land of Youth* (Dublin, 1896).

Ó Gallchobhair, T., 'Bruighean Bheag na h-Almhaine', in Triúr Cómhdhalta do Chuallacht Chuilm Cille, *Gadaidhe Géar na Geamh-oidhche*, 3–13.

— 'Bruighean Chéise Corainn', in Triúr Cómhdhalta do Chuallacht Chuilm Cille, *Gadaidhe Géar Geamh-oidhche*, 69–80.

O'Grady, S.H., *Silva Gadelica*, 2 vols (London, 1892).

— 'Toruigheacht Dhiarmuda agus Ghrainne', in idem (ed.), *Transactions of the Ossianic Society for the Year 1855. Vol. III. Toruigheacht Dhiarmuda agus Ghrainne* (Dublin, 1857) 1–211.

Ó hÓgáin, D., 'Fionn Féin — Pearsa agus Idéal', in Ó Fiannachta (ed.), *An Fhiannaíocht*, 144–63.

— *Fionn mac Cumhaill: Images of the Gaelic Hero* (Dublin, 1988).

— 'Magic Attributes of the Hero in Fenian Lore', in Almqvist, Ó Catháin and Ó Héalaí (eds), *The Heroic Process*, 207–42.

Ó hUiginn, R., 'Captain Somhairle and His Books Revisited', in P. Ó Macháin (ed.), *The Book of the O'Conor Don: Essays on an Irish Manuscript* (Dublin, 2010) 88–102.

— 'Duanaire Finn', in Ó Fiannachta (ed.), *An Fhiannaíocht*, 47–68.

— '*Duanaire Finn*: Patron and Text', in Carey (ed.), *Duanaire Finn: Reassessments*, 79–106.

— '*Fiannaigheacht*, Family, Faith and Fatherland', in Arbuthnot and Parsons (eds), *The Gaelic Finn Tradition*, 151–62.

— 'Somhairle Mac Domhnaill agus *Duanaire Finn*', in P. Breatnach, C. Breatnach and M. Ní Urdail (eds), *Léann Lámhscríbhinní Lobháin: The Louvain Manuscript Heritage*, Éigse: Foilseachán 1 (Dublin, 2007) 42–53.

O'Kearney, N., 'The Battle of Gabhra: Garristown in the County of Dublin, Fought A.D. 283', in idem (ed.), *Transactions of the Ossianic Society, for the Year 1853. Vol. 1. Battle of Gabhra* (Dublin, 1854) 10–161.

— 'Feis Tighe Chonain Chinn-Shleibhe; or, The Festivities at the House of Conan of Ceann-Sleibhe, in the County of Clare', in idem (ed.), *Transactions of the Ossianic Society for the Year 1854. Vol. II. Feis Tighe Chonain* (Dublin, 1855) 117–99.

O'Keeffe, J.G., 'A Prophecy of Find', in J. Fraser, P. Grosjean and J.G. O'Keeffe (cds), *Irish Texts*, 5 vols (London: 1931–4) iii, 43–4.

— 'A Prophecy on the High-kingship of Ireland', J. Fraser, P. Grosjean and J.G. O'Keeffe (eds), *Irish Texts*, 5 vols (London: 1931–4) v, 39–41.

O'Kelly, J.J., *Leabhar na Laoitheadh* (Dublin, 1911).

O'Looney, B., '*Tír na nÓg*: The Land of Youth', in J. O'Daly (ed.), *Transactions of the Ossianic Society for the Year 1856. Vol. IV. Laoithe Fiannuigheachta* (Dublin, 1859) 227–79.

Ó Macháin, P., 'Aonghus Ó Callanáin, Leabhar Leasa Móir agus an *Agallamh Bheag*', in Doyle and Murray (eds), *In Dialogue with the Agallamh*, 144–63.

Ó Muircheartaigh, P., '*Fin as Ossian* Revisited: A Manx Ballad in Bellanagare and its Significance', *Zeitschrift für celtische Philologie* 63 (2016) 95–127.

Ó Muirigh, C. [K. Murray], 'Fionn i nDiaidh na Ríthe: *Úathad mé a Temraig A-nocht*', in E. Mac Carthaigh and J. Uhlich (eds), *Féilscríbhinn do Chathal Ó Háinle* (Indreabhán, 2012) 769–86.

Ó Muraíle, N., 'Agallamh na Seanórach', in Ó Fiannachta (ed.), *An Fhiannaíocht*, 96–127.

— *Leabhar Mór na nGenealach: The Great Book of Irish Genealogies, Com-*

piled (1645–66) by Dubhaltach Mac Fhirbhisigh, 5 vols (Dublin, 2003).

— (ed.), Mícheál Ó Cléirigh, His Associates and St Anthony's College, Louvain (Dublin, 2008).

Ó Murchadha, D., Lige Guill: The Grave of Goll. A Fenian Poem from the Book of Leinster, Irish Texts Society 62 (London, 2009).

O'Rahilly, C., Cath Finntrágha: Edited from MS. Rawlinson B 487, Mediaeval and Modern Irish Series 20 (Dublin, 1962).

— Táin Bó Cúalnge from the Book of Leinster, Irish Texts Society Series 49 (London, 1967); also published outside the series (Dublin, 1967).

— Táin Bó Cúailnge: Recension 1 (Dublin, 1976).

O'Rahilly, T.F., Early Irish History and Mythology (Dublin, 1946).

Ó Síocháin, T., 'Translating Find and the Phantoms into Modern Irish', in T. Birkett and K. March-Lyons (eds), From Eald to New: Translating Early Medieval Poetry for the 21st Century (Woodbridge, forthcoming).

Parsons, G., 'Acallam na Senórach as Prosimetrum', Proceedings of the Harvard Celtic Colloquium 24–5 (2004–5) 86–100.

— 'Breaking the Cycle? Accounts of the Death of Finn', in Arbuthnot and Parsons (eds), Gaelic Finn Tradition, 81–96.

— 'The Narrative Voice in Acallam na Senórach', in Doyle and Murray (eds), In Dialogue with the Agallamh, 109–24.

— Review of Carey (ed.), Duanaire Finn: Reassessments, Cambrian Medieval Celtic Studies 55 (2008) 70–2.

— 'Revisiting Almu in Middle Irish Texts', in E. Boyle and D. Hayden (eds), Authorities and Adaptations: The Reworking and Transmission of Textual Sources in the Middle Ages (Dublin, 2015) 211–31.

— 'The Structure of Acallam na Senórach', Cambrian Medieval Celtic Studies 55 (Summer 2008) 11–40.

— 'Whitley Stokes, Standish Hayes O'Grady and Acallam na Senórach', in E. Boyle and P. Russell (eds), The Tripartite Life of Whitley Stokes (1830–1909) (Dublin, 2011) 185–95.

Pennington, W., 'The Little Colloquy', Philological Quarterly 9, ii (1930) 97–110.

Poppe, E., Of Cycles and Other Critical Matters: Some Issues in Medieval Irish Literary History and Criticism, E.C. Quiggin Memorial Lecture 9 (Cambridge, 2008).

Power, M., 'Cnucha Cnoc os Cionn Life', Zeitschrift für celtische Philologie 11 (1917) 39–55.

Quiggin, E.C., Poems from the Book of the Dean of Lismore, ed. J. Fraser (Cambridge, 1937).

Roe, H., 'Acallamh na Senórach: The Confluence of Lay and Clerical Oral Traditions', in C.J. Byrne, M. Harry and P. Ó Siadhail (eds), Celtic Languages and Celtic Peoples: Proceedings of the Second North American Congress of Celtic Studies Held in Halifax August 16–19, 1989 (Halifax NS, 1992) 331–46.

— 'The Acallam: The Church's Eventual Acceptance of the Cultural Inheritance of Pagan Ireland', in S. Sheehan, J. Findon and W. Follett (eds), Gablánach in Scélaigecht: Celtic Studies in Honour of Ann Dooley

(Dublin, 2013) 103–15.

Ross, A., 'Esus et les "Trois Grues"', *Études Celtiques* 9 (1960) 405–38.

Ross, N., *Heroic Ballads from the Book of the Dean of Lismore*, Scottish Gaelic Texts Society 3 (Edinburgh, 1939).

Royal Irish Academy, *The Book of Leinster, Sometime Called the Book of Glendalough ... with Introduction, Analysis of Contents, and Index by Robert Atkinson* (Dublin, 1880).

Sçavant Irlandois [pseudonym of J. O'Brien / S. Ó. Briain (Bishop of Cloyne and Ross)], 'Mémoire de M. de C. à Messieurs les Auteurs du Journal des Sçavans, au sujet des poëmes de M. Macpherson', *Journal des Sçavans pour l'année M. DCC. LXIV*, 277–92, 353–62, 408–17, 537–55, 604–17, 845–57.

Schlüter, D., '"For the Entertainment of Lords and Commons of Later Times": Past and Remembrance in *Acallam na Senórach*', *Celtica* 26 (2010) 146–60.

Scowcroft, R.M., 'On Liminality in the Fenian Cycle', Review of J.F. Nagy, *The Wisdom of the Outlaw*, Cambridge Medieval Celtic Studies 13 (Summer 1987) 97–100.

Seabhac, An [pseudonym of P. Ó Siochfhradha], *Laoithe na Féinne* (Áth Cliath, 1941).

— *Tóraidheacht an Ghiolla Dheacair* (Corcaigh, 1939).

Sharpe, R., 'Hiberno-Latin *Laicus*, Irish *Láech* and the Devil's Men', *Ériu* 30 (1979) 75–92.

Simms, K. 'Gaelic Warfare in the Middle Ages', in T. Bartlett and K. Jeffery (eds), *A Military History of Ireland* (Cambridge, 1996) 99–115.

Smith, J., *Galic Antiquities: Consisting of A History of the Druids, Particularly those of Caledonia; A Dissertation on the Authenticity of the Poems of Ossian; and A Collection of Ancient Poems, Translated from the Galic of Ullin, Ossian, Orran, &c.* (Edinburgh, 1780).

— *Sean Dana; le Oisian, Orran, Ulann, &c. Ancient Poems of Ossian, Orran, Ullin, &c.* (Edinburgh, 1787).

— *Urnaighean arson Theaghlaichean, &c, agus Laoidhean / Prayers for Families, &c., with a Collection of Hymns in Gaelic* (Glasgow, 1808; reprints Glasgow 1839, 1853; and Edinburgh, no date).

Stafford, F., *The Sublime Savage: A Study of James Macpherson and The Poems of Ossian* (Edinburgh, 1988).

Stern, L.C., 'Die Bekehrung der Fianna', *Zeitschrift für celtische Philologie* 5 (1905) 179–83.

— 'Fiannsruth [aus Yellow Book of Lecan 325a mit Uebersetzung]', *Zeitschrift für celtische Philologie* 1 (1897) 471–3.

— 'Le Manuscrit Irlandais de Leide', *Revue Celtique* 13 (1892) 1–31.

— (trans. J.L. Robertson), 'Ossianic Heroic Poetry', *Transactions of the Gaelic Society of Inverness* 22 (1900) 257–325 (original 'Die ossianischen Heldenlieder', *Zeitschrift für vergleichende Litteraturgeschichte* 8 (1895) 51–86, 143–74).

— 'Eine ossianische Ballade aus dem XII. Jahrhundert', in K. Meyer, L.C. Stern, R. Thurneysen, F. Sommer, W. Foy, A. Leskien, K. Brugmann and

E. Windisch (eds), *Festschrift Whitley Stokes: zum siebzigsten Geburts-tage am 28. Februar 1900* (Leipzig, 1900) 7–19.

Stokes, W., 'Acallamh na Senórach', in E. Windisch and W. Stokes (eds), *Irische Texte mit Wörterbuch*, iv, 1 (Leipzig, 1900) 1–438.

— 'The Annals of Tigernach', *Revue Celtique* 16 (1895) 374–419; 17 (1896) 6–33, 79–223, 337–420; 18 (1897) 9–59, 150–97, 268–303, 374–90; reprint in 2 vols (Lampeter, 1993).

— 'The Colloquy of the Two Sages', *Revue Celtique* 26 (1905) 4–64.

— 'Find and the Phantoms', *Revue Celtique* 7 (1886) 289–307.

— 'On the Calendar of Oengus', *Transactions of the Royal Irish Academy* 1 (1880), separately numbered.

— 'Zimmeriana', *Revue Celtique* 9 (1888) 97–104.

Thanisch, E., 'What the Butlers Saw: *Acallam na Senórach* and its Marginalia in the Book of the White Earl', *Aiste* 4 (2014) 35–57.

Thomson, D.S., 'A Catalogue and Indexes of the Ossianic Ballads in the McLagan MSS', *Scottish Gaelic Studies* 8 (1958) 177–224.

— *The Gaelic Sources of Macpherson's 'Ossian'*, Aberdeen University Studies 130 (Edinburgh, 1952; reprint 1973).

— 'Heroic Ballad Versions from Glen Urquhart', in An Comunn Gaidh-ealach and The Gaelic Society of Inverness (eds), *Sar Ghaidheal: Essays in Memory of Rory Mackay* (Inverness, [1986]) 102–5.

— 'James Macpherson: The Gaelic Dimension', in F. Stafford and H. Gaskill (eds), *From Gaelic to Romantic: Ossianic Translations*, Studies in Comparative Literature 15 (Amsterdam and Atlanta, 1998) 17–26.

— 'Macpherson's *Ossian*: Ballads to Epics', in Almqvist, Ó Catháin and Ó Héalaí (eds), *The Heroic Process*, 243–64.

— 'Some Bogus Gaelic Literature', *Transactions of the Gaelic Society of Glasgow* 5 (1958) 172–88.

Thomson, R.L., *Foirm na n-Urrnuidheadh: John Carswell's Gaelic Trans-lation of the Book of Common Order*, Scottish Gaelic Texts Society 11 (Edinburgh, 1970).

Thurneysen, R., 'Tochmarc Ailbe "Das Werben um Ailbe"', *Zeitschrift für celtische Philologie* 13 (1921) 251–82, 297–8 (corrigenda).

Torna [pseudonym of T. Ó Donnchadha], *Filidheacht Fiannaigheachta* (Corcaigh, no date).

— *Filíocht Fiannaíochta* (Corcaigh, 1954).

Triúr Cómhdhalta do Chuallacht Chuilm Cille [T. Ó Gallchobhair, P. Ua Cuain and T. Mac Giolla Fhionnáin], *Gadaidhe Géar na Geamh-oidhche. I. I n-a bhfuilid suim mhór d'eachtraibh ⁊ d'imtheachtaibh Fhinn ⁊ na Féinne go foir-leathan ⁊ do sgéaltaibh eile nach iad* (Baile Átha Cliath, 1915).

Ua Cuain, P., 'Tóraigheacht Shaidhbhe Inghine Eoghain Óig', in Triúr Cómhdhalta do Chuallacht Chuilm Cille, *Gadaidhe Géar na Geamh-oidhche*, 15–46.

Ua hÓgáin, S. and S. Laoide (eds), *Teacht ⁊ Imtheacht an Ghiolla Dheacair ⁊ Tóruigheacht Chonáin ⁊ a Chuidheachtan* (Baile Átha Cliath, 1905).

van Kranenburg, M., '"Oenach indiu luid in rí": An Edition of the Three

Known Versions of "Today the King Went to a Fair" or *Finn and the Phantoms*: with Translation and Textual Notes', unpublished M.A. thesis (University of Utrecht, 2008).

von Harold, [Edmond] Baron, *Die Gedichte Ossian's* [sic] *eines alten celtischen Helden und Barden*, 3 vols (Düsseldorf, 1775).

Walsh, P., 'Captain Somhairle MacDonnell and His Books', in idem, *Irish Chiefs and Leaders*, ed. C. O Lochlainn (Dublin, 1960) 110–40.

White, N., *Compert Mongáin and Three Other Early Mongán Tales*, Maynooth Medieval Irish Texts 5 (Maynooth, 2006).

Wilson, C.H., *Poems Translated from the Irish Language into the English* (Dublin, 1792).

Windisch, E., 'Drei Gedichte aus der Finnsage', in W. Stokes (ed.), *Irische Texte mit Wörterbuch*, i (Leipzig, 1880) 146–64.

Yeats, W.B., *The Wanderings of Oisin and Other Poems* (London, 1889).

Young, M., 'Antient Gaelic Poems respecting the Race of the Fians, collected in the Highlands of Scotland in the Year 1784', *Transactions of the Royal Irish Academy* 1 (1787) 43–119.

Zimmer, H., 'Keltische Beiträge III. Weitere nordgermanische Einflüsse in der ältesten Ueberlieferung der irischen Heldensage', *Zeitschrift für deutsches Alterthum und deutsche Litteratur* 35 (1891) 1–172.

— 'Ossin und Oskar. Ein weiteres Zeugnis für den Ursprung der irisch-gälischen Finn (-Ossian-) Sage in der Vikingerzeit', *Zeitschrift für deutsches Alterthum und deutsche Litteratur* 35 (1891) 252–5.

— Review of H. d'Arbois de Jubainville, *Essai d'un catalogue de la littérature épique de l'Irlande*, *Göttingische gelehrte Anzeigen* (1887) 169–73, 184–93.

Index

Made in the USA
Columbia, SC
17 July 2017